FIGHTER COMMAND
1939-45

FIGHTER COMMAND
1939-45

IAN CARTER

PHOTOGRAPHS FROM THE IMPERIAL WAR MUSEUM

This page :
An immaculate formation of No 111 Squadron Hurricanes, January 1938.
'Treble One' was chosen to introduce the new monoplane fighter into RAF
service, the first aircraft arriving at Northolt in December 1937. The traditional
techniques employed in the manufacture of the Hurricane made for rapid
production, and by September 1939 16 squadrons had been equipped.
HU 68334

CONTENTS

First published 2002

ISBN 0 7110 2842 7

Published by Ian Allan Publishing

an imprint of Ian Allan Publishing Ltd, Hersham, Surrey KT12 4RG.
Printed by Ian Allan Printing Ltd, Hersham, Surrey KT12 4RG.

Code: 0205/B3

PREFACE

In the summer of 1940 Royal Air Force Fighter Command won a famous victory over Hitler's Luftwaffe. The Battle of Britain, when several hundred RAF Spitfire and Hurricane pilots ensured national survival, has long been regarded as the RAF's finest hour. Yet the events of 1940, which encompassed stinging defeat in France and Norway as well as supremacy in the skies over southern England, heralded the start of a more protracted struggle. In the years that followed, Fighter Command not only maintained its ceaseless watch on Britain's skies, guarding her cities, ports and coastal convoys, but also conducted an increasingly effective campaign of offensive operations over enemy-occupied Europe. In 1944, when Allied armies returned to France, they did so in conditions of almost complete air superiority, established to a great extent by the fighter squadrons of the RAF. By this date Fighter Command had been split, with much of its strength assigned to a new formation, the 2nd Tactical Air Force, whose mission was to support the armies on the Continent. As British and Canadian troops advanced, the fighter-bombers of 2nd TAF were in the vanguard, ready to pulverise the enemy's ground forces and the infrastructure that supported them.

The broadening role of the RAF placed great demands on its aircraft, and it was fortunate indeed that Fighter Command possessed some of the war's truly great designs. The Supermarine Spitfire, forever the symbol of 1940, would also bear the brunt of the daylight offensive in the mid-war years. Thanks to its astounding capacity for development, the Spitfire was able to match the temporary ascendancy of the Luftwaffe's Focke-Wulf FW190, and through succeeding marks maintain its place in the front line until the end of the war. The Hawker Typhoon, planned as a defensive 'bomber destroyer', instead won fame as perhaps the most effective — and certainly the most feared — ground-attack aircraft on either side. The de Havilland Mosquito, without peer as a precision bomber, was also undoubtedly the finest night-fighter of the war. Another aircraft of war-winning importance was the American-built Mustang, which, in its Merlin-engined guise, finally gave UK-based squadrons an air superiority fighter with the 'legs' to reach deep into Germany itself.

The nature of air fighting changed dramatically as the war progressed. As Germany's fortunes ebbed opportunities to engage the Luftwaffe in air-to-air combat declined, and the role of the fighter in ground-support operations became ever more important. But if the job was changing, the exhilaration, stress and danger of operational flying remained constant. Fighter Command never suffered anything like the blood-letting endured by Bomber Command, but the early years of the cross-Channel offensive were especially costly, and even at the very end, when the Luftwaffe was often conspicuous by its absence, losses were far from insignificant. The Spitfire pilot of 1945, screaming in to strafe a German goods train through a wall of flak, required no less courage, skill and luck than his predecessor of 1940, frantically trying to shake off a pursuing Me109 high over Kent.

In this book I have gathered together a selection of photographs held in the archives of the Imperial War Museum. Most were taken by RAF photographers on official assignments; others are the work of private individuals or the press. I hope that many will be new to most readers; the Museum's collection is a rich source, and where possible I have selected images that offer a fresh view of familiar subjects. The captions are based on the original photographers' notes, supplemented by official records, published reference works and personal accounts. I have tried to paint a broad picture of RAF fighter operations over Britain and the Continent, including the activities not only of Fighter Command itself but also of the squadrons sent to France at the beginning of the war, and later, those of 2nd TAF during the campaign in northwest Europe. Some of the famous 'aces' and fighter leaders will appear in the following pages, alongside representatives of a much larger group — that great mass of squadron pilots who lacked either the ability or opportunity (but never the will) to shoot down enemy aircraft in large numbers. This book is also about the ground echelons, the 'Many' of Fighter Command. They were the fitters and riggers, the armourers and radio specialists, the drivers and medics, and those in a host of other trades — men and women to whom so much is also owed.

ACKNOWLEDGEMENTS

Extracts from a number of works are reproduced with the kind permission of the publishers: *Wing Leader* by Air Vice-Marshal J. E. Johnson © 1956 (Crécy Publishing); *Dennis 'Hurricane' David: My Autobiography* by Dennis David (Grub Street Publishing); *Fighter Pilot* by Paul Richey (Pen & Sword Books). Permission to reproduce material from the Official History (*The Defence of the United Kingdom* by B. Collier), and from *Royal Air Force 1939-45* by Denis Richards and Hilary Saunders, was supplied by the Controller of Her Majesty's Stationery Office. All the photographs in this book are reproduced with the permission of the Imperial War Museum; copies are available on application to the Photograph Archive. I am pleased to acknowledge the expert assistance of my colleagues in the Museum, especially photographers Richard Bayford and Gordon McLeod. Jerry Scutts and Ray Sturtivant provided help with a number of references. Special thanks go to my wife Marian, who worked so hard checking text and captions. As with my previous work on Bomber Command, the many RAF veterans I have met and corresponded with over recent years have provided information and inspiration for this modest photographic tribute. It is to them that the book is dedicated.

Above: Pilot Officer Peter Kells, the pilot of a Blenheim IF of No 29 Squadron climbs into his cockpit at the start of another night patrol from Coleby Grange. Lincolnshire, October 1940. No 29 was one of six Blenheim squadrons engaged in night-fighting duties at this time. Few aircraft were fitted with radar, and fewer still had any success against enemy bombers in the darkness over Britain. **CH 1584**

INTRODUCTION

'The best defence of the country is the Fear of the Fighter. If we are strong in fighters we should probably never be attacked in force.'

(Air Chief Marshal Sir Hugh Dowding, 1939)

Royal Air Force Fighter Command officially came into being on 14 July 1936 when its first Air Officer Commanding-in-Chief, Air Marshal (later Air Chief Marshal) Sir Hugh Dowding, took up his new post at Bentley Priory, near Stanmore in Middlesex. Charged with the aerial defence of the United Kingdom, Fighter Command also had operational control of the Army's anti-aircraft batteries and searchlight units. It was one of a number of functional commands (the others included Bomber, Coastal and Training) which replaced the existing Air Defence of Great Britain, the complex umbrella organisation hitherto responsible for the static defences and all home-based squadrons, whatever their role. The new system would, it was hoped, be better able to cope with the rapid expansion of the RAF that was now taking place as Britain sought to counter the menace of Hitler's Germany.

Moves to increase the size of the RAF had been set in train 13 years before, at a time when it was discovered that, across the Channel, France's *Armée de l'Air* comprised some 600 aircraft. In contrast, the once mighty RAF had been allowed to dwindle to just 25 squadrons, most of which were stationed overseas; fewer than 40 aircraft were based in Britain. Alarmed by this disparity, the Government agreed in 1923 to expand the Home Defence Air Force to 52 squadrons, regarded as the minimum requirement for the defence of London and other key targets. However, the prevailing climate of financial stringency and growing hopes for international disarmament meant that this first phase of expansion progressed all too slowly. Indeed, the very survival of the RAF as an independent service was called into question, resolved only by the efforts of its 'founding father', Lord Trenchard, to promote the service's vital — and relatively inexpensive — role in external policing duties throughout the Empire. In this he succeeded, but the continuing economic retrenchment of the late 1920s and early 1930s left the RAF short in numbers and with a woefully inadequate level of equipment.

By the mid-1930s it was Nazi Germany that posed the greatest threat to Britain's security — a fact that could no longer be ignored, even by the most idealistic of governments. The response was a succession of eight expansion schemes, intended to rectify the RAF's deficiencies and achieve parity in numbers with Hitler's Luftwaffe. Fortunately the institutions and organisational structure of Britain's air arm were now in place, thanks to the work of Lord Trenchard during the preceding decade, but there was a great deal of ground to make up in terms of front-line equipment. When Dowding took up his post as Commander-in-Chief in mid-1936, he had at his disposal a mere 18 squadrons, all still equipped with biplane fighters little different from those that had been in service in 1918. The Bristol Bulldog, Hawker Fury and Gloster Gauntlet all had open cockpits, fixed undercarriages and twin .303in Vickers machine-guns firing through the propeller arc. The Hawker Demon was an unnecessary revival of the RAF's two-seat fighter concept from World War 1. A new type about to enter service, the Gloster Gladiator, took biplane development about as far as it would go, but represented only a marginal improvement on existing designs. Yet dramatic change was waiting in the wings. The prototypes of a new generation of fast, eight-gun monoplane fighters — the revolutionary Hawker Hurricane and Supermarine Spitfire — had already flown, and the race to get these two advanced aircraft into squadron service would form the most vital element in the story of Fighter Command during the remaining years of peace.

Although rapid expansion had at last been set in motion, the accent at first was on bombers rather than fighters, a reflection of the Air Staff's long-cherished doctrine — espoused most forcefully by Trenchard himself — that the RAF was essentially an offensive force, and that a strong bomber force was in itself the best form of defence. Little thought was given to the strategic value of the aircraft chosen, nor care taken to provide for sufficient reserves, since the object was to deter Germany's ambitions by matching her own air force, plane for plane. Hitler's moves to annexe the Sudetenland in Czechoslovakia in the summer of 1938, and the ensuing rise in international tension, revealed serious shortcomings in the RAF's preparedness for war. In September, at the height of the Munich Crisis, Fighter Command could mobilise only 30 squadrons, most still equipped with biplanes. Five squadrons had converted to the new Hurricane, and even a handful of Spitfires had trickled into service, but it was a force not yet ready by any means to take on the perceived might of the Luftwaffe.

One person who fought continually against the Air Staff's obsession with bombers was the C-in-C of Fighter Command, and there can be little doubt as to Dowding's pivotal role in preparing the RAF for the defensive battle it would soon have to face. Although austere and difficult to know, 'Stuffy' Dowding was a visionary who worked tirelessly to expand and modernise his squadrons, and to create an integrated ground-to-air command structure with which to maximise their effectiveness. He was especially attuned to the potential of new aircraft, most notably the Spitfire and Hurricane, as well as the benefits from advances in technology. In his earlier capacity on the Air Council as Air Member for Supply and Research, he had backed Robert Watson-Watt's early scientific experiments with 'Radio Direction Finding' (RDF — later known as radar), and then ensured that a chain of RDF stations was built along the southern and eastern coastline of Britain. Aided by the civilian-manned Observer Corps, which visually tracked and reported all friendly and hostile aircraft movements, radar would prove of inestimable value when put to the test in 1940.

Valuable progress was made in the breathing space bought by appeasement at Munich, and Fighter Command was gradually transformed. Spitfire and Hurricane production rose sharply, and by the summer of 1939 a reserve of 200 fighters had been assembled. 'Group pools' (later known as 'operational training units') were established to teach raw pilots how to handle the new aircraft, a task hitherto carried out by the squadrons themselves. However, despite the growing awareness of the need for a strong fighter force to stop the enemy's much-feared 'knockout blow' from the air, Dowding was obliged to fight tooth-and-nail to prevent the dispersal of his squadrons. The expected commitment of an expeditionary force to France meant that he was forced to reserve four Hurricane squadrons for this enterprise, and earmark a further six for later deployment.

Another call on Dowding's minimal resources came from the Admiralty, which requested that squadrons be assigned to the defence of coastal convoys, and the Home Fleet's base at Scapa Flow in the Far North.

At the beginning of September 1939 Fighter Command had a total of 37 operational fighter squadrons, organised into three geographic defence areas or 'groups'. In the South was No 11 Group with 19 squadrons; No 12 Group had 10 squadrons to defend the Midlands and East Anglia; and No 13 Group took care of northern England and Scotland with eight squadrons. This force (which included the four squadrons earmarked for France) was still well short of the 46 squadrons that Dowding himself regarded as the absolute minimum necessary, but at least three-quarters of them were now wholly or partly equipped with Spitfires and Hurricanes. More squadrons were forming, and the process of expansion and re-equipment was continuing apace when Hitler's armies invaded Poland, and Britain was once again plunged into war.

Above: The Bristol Bulldog entered service in May 1929, and was the most widely used RAF fighter until the mid-1930s. For much of this time, however, its top speed of 178mph was below that of many of the RAF's own light bomber types. When Fighter Command was created in July 1936 Bulldogs still equipped four squadrons, but these soon converted to Gauntlets and Gladiators. These No 3 Squadron aircraft are seen taxiing at Hendon in July 1929. **H(AM) 74**

Above: Hawker Furies of No 25 Squadron, 1935. The elegant Fury entered service in 1931, and was the first RAF fighter to exceed 200mph in level flight. It was designed as a specialised interceptor, able to climb rapidly to the height of attacking bomber formations. The Mk II, which had a more powerful engine, did not become operational until 1936. **HU 3664**

Above: A Hawker Demon of No 23 Squadron at the RAF Review at Mildenhall, July 1935. The Demon was an adaptation of the Hart light bomber and entered service in 1931. In later versions, named Turret Demons, the rear Lewis gun was operated hydraulically and fitted with a segmented armoured shield for the gunner. The RAF's obsolete two-seat fighter concept was perpetuated in the Demon's replacement, the Boulton Paul Defiant. **HU 3671**

Above: Gloster Gauntlets of No 19 Squadron, also at Mildenhall in July 1935. The Gauntlet was introduced in May of that year, and with a top speed of 230mph was appreciably faster than its predecessor, the Bristol Bulldog. However, its open cockpit, bulky air-cooled radial engine and armament of only two fuselage-mounted machine-guns all dated back to World War 1. **HU 26040**

Above: Last of the RAF's biplane fighters, the Gloster Gladiator entered service in February 1937. With four Browning machine-guns, an enclosed cockpit and a top speed of over 250mph, the Gladiator was an advance on the Gauntlet and was still in limited front-line service at the outbreak of war. These are aircraft of No 72 Squadron, lined up at Farnborough during the 1937 Air Exercises. **H(AM) 192**

Above: First of the many — K5083, the prototype Hawker Hurricane. Sidney Camm's Hurricane originated as a monoplane development of the Hawker Fury, employing tried-and-tested methods of airframe construction. A 1934 Air Ministry specification was written around the proposed new design, which promised a top speed of well over 300mph and could accommodate a battery of eight machine-guns. The prototype took to the air in November 1935, and a production contract for 600 aircraft followed in June 1936. **MH 5745**

Left:
The prototype Boulton Paul Defiant, K8310, which first flew in August 1937. Intended to supplant the Hawker Demon, the Defiant stemmed from a 1935 Air Ministry requirement for a two-seat interceptor built around a four-gun, power-operated turret. No forward-firing armament was carried. The result was an attractive aircraft, with excellent flying qualities, but mock combats against Hurricanes revealed the sluggish Defiant to be a poor match for conventional single-seaters. **MH 5507**

Above: No 19 Squadron displays its Supermarine Spitfires at Duxford, 4 May 1939. All aircraft have the early two-bladed, fixed-pitch propellers. Like the Hurricane, Reginald Mitchell's Spitfire started out as a private venture, attracting Air Ministry attention once its potential was appreciated. Unlike the Hawker fighter, the Spitfire had an advanced all-metal monocoque airframe, which slowed up production until the required manufacturing techniques were mastered. The aircraft first flew in March 1936, and entered service with No 19 Squadron in August 1938. **HU 48148**

Left:
Spitfire Is of No 65 Squadron at Hornchurch, summer 1939. By the outbreak of war, Spitfires were on strength with 11 Fighter Command squadrons. The three-bladed, variable-pitch propellers now fitted were a major improvement, reducing the take-off run and improving the aircraft's top speed and rate of climb. Within a year, constant-speed propellers — which automatically matched blade pitch to engine speed — had been fitted to all aircraft. **HU 68053**

> *'Four fighter squadrons to defend the entire British Expeditionary Force! It was absurd. But at least we were not afraid to fight and if necessary to die, and we were confident we would give a good account of ourselves.'*
>
> (Wing Commander Paul Richey DFC and Bar)

In accordance with plans agreed earlier by the British and French governments, the outbreak of war saw the movement of a substantial number of RAF aircraft to France. Fighter Command was immediately denuded of four squadrons of Hurricanes (Nos 1, 73, 85 and 87), which were despatched as part of the Air Component of the British Expeditionary Force (BEF). Their role was to cover the activities of the Component's reconnaissance and army co-operation squadrons. Dowding had fought vigorously against sending a fighter contingent, fearing that any squadrons sent to the Continent were as good as lost — he needed every plane and pilot for home defence. Fortunately, however, the expected mass German aerial assault on Britain, and on London in particular, did not materialise. Instead, the Luftwaffe limited itself to forays against merchant shipping and the Home Fleet in the North. These early actions resulted in Fighter Command's first aerial victories of the war, beginning on 16 October when Spitfires of Nos 602 and 603 Squadrons shot down two Junkers Ju88s over the Firth of Forth. The next day, a trio of Gladiators from No 607 Squadron destroyed a Dornier Do18 flying boat off the Scottish coast, and on 21 October No 46 Squadron Hurricanes downed four Heinkel He115 seaplanes during a convoy patrol off the East Coast.

Elsewhere, the period of relative inactivity — soon to become known as the 'Phoney War' — gave Fighter Command valuable months to continue its growth and re-equipment. October was a busy month, and saw the formation of 18 new squadrons. Owing to shortages of Spitfires and Hurricanes, these embryo units were equipped at first with a variety of lesser types, mostly Gladiators and twin-engined Blenheim IFs, but some had to make do with Fairey Battle light bombers, obsolete Gauntlets and even Magister trainers. One of the new squadrons, No 264, was chosen to introduce a new front-line type into service, the Boulton Paul Defiant. Designed principally as a bomber-destroyer, this two-seat, single-engined aircraft carried all its armament in a power-operated gun turret behind the pilot. Dowding was opposed to the Defiant, believing that it represented an evolutionary dead-end in fighter design, and later service would indeed reveal the aircraft's fatal inadequacies. The RDF network also needed fine-tuning, a fact most dramatically demonstrated on 6 September by the notorious 'Battle of Barking Creek', when technical problems and reporting errors saw two groups of RAF fighters mistakenly vectored on to each other over East Anglia. In the blinding sun's glare, correct visual identification between the two formations of aircraft was impossible, and a Hurricane pilot of No 56 Squadron was shot down and killed by two No 74 Squadron Spitfires.

In France it was not until the end of October that RAF Hurricanes began skirmishing with the enemy, mainly against reconnaissance aircraft which relied on cloud cover to make good their escape when challenged by British or French fighters. On 30 October Pilot Officer Peter 'Boy' Mould of No 1 Squadron 'chalked up' the first victory of the RAF's French-based fighter squadrons when he shot down a Dornier Do17. Not to be outdone, No 73 Squadron opened its scoring on 8 November, when Flying Officer Edgar 'Cobber' Kain claimed another Dornier. Both squadrons were now operating in support of the Fairey Battle light bombers of the Advanced Air Striking Force (AASF), based near Rheims, whose task was to undertake reconnaissance flights over the Franco-German border. French fighter squadrons, originally charged with their defence, had failed to provide adequate cover for the vulnerable Battles. The two remaining Air Component fighter units, Nos 85 and 87 Squadrons, stationed further north near the Belgian border, achieved their first victories in November.

Dowding lost two more of his squadrons in mid-November, when Nos 607 and 615, equipped with Gladiators, were despatched to the Air Component. At home, enemy activity against the naval bases at Rosyth and Scapa Flow forced the Home Fleet to sail to safer anchorages on the West Coast, but the Luftwaffe nevertheless continued its reconnaissance flights and attacks on East Coast convoys and shore installations. On 20 November No 11 Group, covering the southern half of the country, finally got the chance to engage the enemy, with Spitfires of No 74 Squadron shooting down a Dornier Do17 off Southend. On the following day another reconnaissance Dornier was brought down over the Channel, this time by No 79 Squadron Hurricanes. Blenheim IFs of Nos 25 and 601 Squadrons were also in action at the end of November when they struck in daylight at German seaplane bases on Borkum in the Frisian Islands, but their efforts failed to inflict any significant damage.

The last weeks of the year were characterised by limited aerial activity, as flying was restricted by the onset of winter weather. At least it was now clear that there would be no German assault in the West before Christmas, and the Phoney War looked set to continue into the New Year. Aircraft production was gradually getting into gear, but time was needed to complete the re-equipment of the new squadrons, which remained far from operational. By the end of the year Fighter Command had claimed the destruction of 29 enemy aircraft over France and Britain, for the loss of only a handful of pilots. But these kills had been relatively easy; the distances flown on most Luftwaffe sorties meant that, so far, only unescorted bombers, minelayers

Above: The first German aircraft to crash on British soil was this Heinkel He111, engaged over the Firth of Forth by Spitfires of Nos 602 and 603 Squadrons on 28 October 1939. Pursued at low level by the RAF fighters, the German bomber was riddled by machine-gun fire, which killed two of its crew and wounded another. It crash-landed on a hillside near Haddington, East Lothian, and was the focus of much interest when this photograph was taken the next day. **HU 86587**

and reconnaissance machines had been encountered. It was not until the end of December that RAF fighters met what, for many of them, would be their nemesis.

The Messerschmitt Bf109 (which the RAF almost always referred to as the 'Me'109) was the Luftwaffe's principal single-seat fighter, and had already tangled with French aircraft and RAF bombers. The latest version, the Bf109E-3 (known as the 'Emil'), was armed with two 20mm cannon and two machine-guns. It was comparable in performance to the Spitfire, and superior in many respects to the Hurricane. On 22 December a

quartet of Me109s, led by the leading German ace Werner Mölders, 'bounced' a section of three Hurricanes from No 73 Squadron patrolling near Metz. In typical fashion, the enemy fighters attacked from above, using their superior speed to scythe through the British 'vic' formation, shooting down two aircraft in short order before diving away. The unfortunate recipients of their fire probably died before they knew what was happening. The encounter was a short, sharp exposition of classic Luftwaffe fighter tactics, for which Fighter Command was singularly unprepared. It was a portent of things to come.

Above: This unusual view of a No 85 Squadron Hurricane at Lille-Seclin in November 1939 shows to good effect the fabric-covered outer wings characteristic of early production aircraft. These were chosen initially to ensure a faster rate of production, but were soon substituted for stressed-skin metal wings. Note the Watts fixed-pitch wooden propeller and the gas detection patch painted below the cockpit. **C 460**

Above: No 87 Squadron was also based at Lille-Seclin for much of the so-called 'Phoney War', and the following sequence of photographs was taken there in November 1939. In the first, pilots obligingly run to their machines for a mock 'scramble'. By now some replacement Hurricanes were arriving in France fitted with de Havilland three-bladed variable-pitch propellers, as evident in this photograph. **C 468**

Right:
A Hurricane being refuelled from an Albion triple-hose petrol bowser. The vehicle was designed to service three fighters at once, but this facility was less useful when aircraft were routinely dispersed across their airfield. The Hurricane's 97gal capacity was divided between two main wing tanks and a reserve fuel cell immediately in front of the cockpit. This gave the aircraft a normal operating range of about 440 miles. **C 456**

Right:
Pilots and ground crew gather around the fuselage *Balkenkreuz* from No 87 Squadron's first kill, a Heinkel He111 shot down by Flight Lieutenant Robert Voase-Jeff on 2 November. Pilot Officer Dennis David, who damaged another Heinkel on the same day, autographs the trophy. Watching on the right is a new member of the squadron, Pilot Officer Roland Beamont (in flying helmet, with initials on his Irvin flying jacket), a future ace and famous postwar test-pilot. **C 457**

Left:
Off-duty ground staff listen to the wireless in their billet. Accommodation for RAF personnel in France during the Phoney War varied considerably. Officers were usually put up in private houses or above their messes in local hotels, while airmen might be quartered in barns, garages, disused barrack blocks or even corn silos. Note the beds, constructed from empty petrol tins and planks. **C 464**

Above:
On 6 December 1939 King George VI, with the Duke of Gloucester and Viscount Lord Gort (Commander-in-Chief of the BEF), inspected RAF Air Component units at Lille-Seclin. Here the King greets Squadron Leader J. S. 'Johnny' Dewar, commanding No 87 Squadron, in front of a smart line-up of Hurricanes. Dewar went on to shoot down at least five enemy aircraft during the Battle of France, but was killed in September 1940. **F 2344A**

Right:
Across the rainswept hard-standing from the Hurricanes seen in the previous photograph, the King inspects personnel from No 615 Squadron, Auxiliary Air Force, drawn up in front of one of their Gladiators. A Blenheim IV from one of the Air Component's strategic-reconnaissance squadrons can be seen in the background.
F 2344D

Above: Hurricane pilots of No 73 Squadron entertain a Greek newspaper correspondent at their base at Rouvres, December 1939. Along with No 1 Squadron at Vassincourt, No 73 had been given the task of protecting the vulnerable Fairey Battles of the AASF. For the present, however, their main role was to mount standing patrols against German reconnaissance aircraft. By the end of November the squadron had shot down at least three Dornier Do17s probing French airspace. **C 179**

Left:
Hanging out the washing — though not yet on the Siegfried Line. An RAF airman dries his pyjamas in his billet 'somewhere in France', December 1939. As the first Christmas of the war approached, RAF personnel in France made the best of their surroundings. With the Germans busy elsewhere, they had not been severely tested, but all were aware that the Phoney War would not last forever. **C 87**

1940

'Whatever we did in the air, and no matter how many German aircraft we destroyed, it seemed to make no difference; the German forces kept advancing and seemed invincible. But all the time we were learning from them, for they were the experts.'

(Group Captain Dennis David CBE, DFC and Bar, AFC)

The first two months of the year saw only limited aerial activity, as Europe remained in the grip of one of the coldest winters in living memory. On the western front, troops and airmen alike shivered in their billets, while over Britain the poor flying conditions kept enemy incursions to a minimum. During occasional periods of clearer weather the Luftwaffe mounted reconnaissance sorties and strikes against East Coast convoys, keeping the northern-based RAF squadrons relatively busy. One of the most successful pilots during this period was Squadron Leader Andrew Farquhar, commanding No 602 Squadron, Auxiliary Air Force. He shot down a Heinkel He111 over the Firth of Forth on 9 February, and had a hand in several other victories. By contrast, it was still frustratingly quiet for the squadrons in the South, but on 13 February a lone He111 was detected approaching the Thames Estuary on a reconnaissance flight. Patrolling aircraft from No 54 Squadron were vectored towards the intruder, and shot it into the sea.

Improving weather brought an upsurge in enemy activity in March and April, especially over France where Nos 1 and 73 Squadrons tangled with Me109s and twin-engined Me110s on several occasions. By now a number of pilots in France had got one or more kills, and before March was out 'Cobber' Kain shot down his fifth enemy aircraft, becoming the RAF's first ace of the war.

These early combats were beginning to reveal fatal flaws in RAF tactics. The neat but unwieldy 'bomber-destroying' formations, with aircraft flying in 'vics' of three, one section behind the other, were shown to be terribly vulnerable to the diving tactics of the Luftwaffe fighters. With the emphasis on keeping formation with the leader, RAF pilots had little time to search for the enemy or, more vitally, spot an attack from above and behind. By contrast, the Germans flew in more fluid, mutually supporting pairs, with pilots able to cover each other's blind spot and manœuvre with ease. No 1 Squadron, under its forceful CO, Squadron Leader 'Bull' Halahan, was especially keen to revise its tactics. The unit experimented with formations of five aircraft, the last two being 'tail-end Charlies' whose job was to weave protectively over the rear of the group. The pilots also had their guns harmonised to converge on a spot 250yd ahead of their aircraft, instead of spreading out to 400yd. This concentrated the weight of fire that struck an enemy aircraft, and was later officially approved for all RAF fighters.

April also saw an extension of RAF activity to Norway following the German invasion, which began on the 9th. Fighter Command's initial part in this doomed campaign involved No 263 Squadron, which was despatched aboard the aircraft carrier HMS *Glorious*. The squadron was based on a frozen lake in central Norway, but within days of arriving most of its obsolescent Gladiators were destroyed in bombing attacks, and it was forced to return home. In mid-May No 46 Squadron, flying Hurricanes, joined in the action, and operated alongside a re-equipped No 263 until the final evacuation of British forces in June. The RAF fighters held their own in these desperate weeks and exacted a toll on the Luftwaffe, but by now the Norwegian campaign had become little more than a sideshow to the Battle of France. The final tragedy was the loss of most of the returning squadron personnel, and all their aircraft, when HMS *Glorious*, on which they were embarked, was sunk by the German battle-cruisers *Scharnhorst* and *Gneisenau*. Eighteen pilots from the two squadrons were drowned.

On 10 May Hitler's long-expected assault on the West began. Bypassing the strongly-defended Maginot Line, the initial German attacks were directed through the Netherlands, Belgium and Luxembourg, with paratroops and gliders descending on a host of important canal crossings and strongpoints. The Luftwaffe provided massive support, attacking 70 airfields in France and the Low Countries, including the RAF bases. In compliance with previously agreed plans, British and French troops advanced forwards into Belgium, while RAF light bombers made futile and costly attacks against the advancing German columns. What was not immediately appreciated by the Allied High Command was that the *Blitzkrieg* through the Netherlands and northern Belgium was intended merely to draw in the British and French forces. The main axis of the German assault into France was to the south, through the supposedly impassable Ardennes forest region. The German *Panzers* forced a crossing over the River Meuse at Sedan on 13 May, pushed on westwards and began a major encirclement of the Allied northern armies.

From the beginning, the RAF fighter squadrons found themselves in the thick of the action, and were quickly reinforced. By 12 May four more Hurricane squadrons had flown out to join the six already in the field, to be followed later by elements from other units. The 'dripping tap' that Air Chief Marshal Dowding had long dreaded was now a reality. Despite assurances to the French made by Britain's new Prime Minister, Winston Churchill, Dowding was resolutely opposed to supplying any further fighter reinforcements. On 16 May he sent his now famous letter to the Air Ministry in which he bluntly spelled out the gravity of the situation. With only the equivalent of 36 squadrons left in Britain, he claimed that the loss of any more would leave Fighter Command fatally weakened. He had no doubts about the consequences: '...if the Home Defence Force

Above: Pilots of No 1 Squadron at Vassincourt show off one of their Hurricanes to Mr Mahmoud Abu Fath, a member of the Egyptian Parliament, January 1940. Visits by journalists and VIPs were an unpopular distraction for the squadrons in France, but had to be tolerated as part of the wider propaganda effort. Looking at the camera is Flying Officer Billy Drake, who became a 20-kill ace and survived the war. **C 505**

Left:
For shooting down the first German aircraft to fall to the RAF in France, Flight Lieutenant Robert Voase-Jeff of No 87 Squadron was awarded the Croix de Guerre. He is seen here among a group of French pilots at the ceremony on 3 February 1940, saluting General Vuillemin, the Commander-in-Chief of the French Air Force. Voase-Jeff was killed in action during the Battle of Britain. **C 623**

is drained away in desperate attempts to remedy the situation in France, defeat in France will involve the final, complete and irremediable defeat of this country.' With backing from the Chiefs of Staff Dowding finally got his way, and no further fighters were committed.

Meanwhile, the campaign itself was heading towards its tragic and inevitable conclusion. The French, their will to resist already weakening, had no strategic reserve to plug the huge breach torn by the Germans, and the BEF was retreating towards the Channel coast, constantly harried by the Luftwaffe. The RAF Hurricanes fought tenaciously (pilots were flying up to five or more sorties daily), claiming many of the enemy in the process, but were under constant pressure as they withdrew hastily from one airstrip to another in the face of the German advance. The Messerschmitt pilots had the edge in terms of speed, but learned not to engage in dogfights with the more manoeuvrable Hurricanes at low level. The Hawker fighters, thanks to their traditional construction, were able to absorb terrific punishment and still return to base. However, there was no answer to the enemy's numerical superiority. By 21 May the Air Component Hurricanes had evacuated, leaving only three AASF squadrons, which retreated into central France.

On 26 May Operation 'Dynamo' began as the Royal Navy, heroically assisted by the civilian-manned 'little ships', attempted to evacuate the BEF from Dunkirk. Air Vice-Marshal Park's No 11 Group, with about 200 available aircraft, provided the bulk of the air cover for this enterprise, but eventually all but three of Fighter Command's squadrons would be involved at one time or another. The odds were not in their favour. Pilots were forced to operate at least 50 miles from their bases, and sometimes outside the range of radar and radio control from England. Baling out usually meant capture, or worse if over the Channel. Attempts to provide constant cover using small standing patrols placed the RAF fighters at a severe disadvantage to the numerically superior Luftwaffe, so it was decided to despatch larger forces comprising two or three squadrons at a time. This offered some sort of parity in numbers with the enemy but could not be maintained continuously, and left gaps in the air cover that the Luftwaffe was quick to exploit. Nevertheless, the RAF fighters were able on many occasions to intercept raiders heading for the beaches, a fact that was not appreciated — perhaps understandably so — by the Army at the time. As a result, many more troops were rescued than was expected, and at least 130 German aircraft were destroyed. For the first time in the war, the Luftwaffe had met its match in the air, but the Dunkirk operation had been a costly drain on Fighter

Below:
An underground dugout serves as the duty office for No 73 Squadron at Rouvres, February 1940. A flying jacket conveniently obscures confidential information on the operations board. The youthful officer second from right is Flying Officer Richard 'Dickie' Martin, who had achieved a certain degree of fame the previous November when he crash-landed his aircraft in Belgium, was interned and then escaped to rejoin his unit. **C 748**

Above: Spitfire Is of No 65 Squadron in a newly constructed blast pen at Hornchurch, late February 1940. The nearest aircraft, K9911/YT-E, has strakes for fitting exhaust shields (to reduce glare at night) on the forward fuselage. None of these aircraft would see out the year — K9911 was shot down by Bf109s over Manston on 8 August, K9907/YT-D was lost near Dover on 8 July, and L1094/YT-H dived into the ground in Northumberland on 4 November, while serving with No 610 Squadron. **HU 86066**

Command's slender resources. During the nine days of the evacuation the RAF lost 113 fighters, and 67 pilots and air gunners.

RAF involvement in France did not end with Dunkirk. Many thousands of British troops remained in France, and further contingents, some recently evacuated from Norway, were despatched to aid the French as the campaign entered its last stages. The three AASF Hurricane squadrons still on the Continent, by now severely under-strength, continued to offer what assistance they could during the retreat westwards, and were reinforced when Nos 17 and 242 Squadrons flew out to join them on 8 June. Support also came from Fighter Command's home-based squadrons, but it was all far too late and served only to further reduce the Command's strength at a critical time. No 43 Squadron had a particularly black day on 7 June when no fewer than seven of its Hurricanes were shot down by Me109s over Amiens. France was on the point of collapse, and another series of British evacuations began, this time from Cherbourg and the Atlantic ports. As their ground echelons sailed with the remnants of the Army, the last RAF fighters were flown out on 18 June. The six weeks of fighting during the Battle of France had cost Fighter Command 386 Hurricanes and 67 Spitfires. At least half of the Hurricanes lost were unserviceable aircraft abandoned during the retreat. Overall, however, the Hurricane had acquitted itself well, and the experience gained by the pilots who survived, especially those who had become aces during those hectic weeks, would prove of inestimable value during the months ahead.

The great and decisive aerial campaign that followed, subsequently known as the Battle of Britain, has in the past been divided up by historians into various overlapping phases, based largely on apparent changes in German objectives and tactics. British and German authorities differ over the precise dates involved, and there is even dispute over when the battle actually started. For the purposes of the campaign medal, the Air Ministry officially decided on 10 July, but this rather arbitrary date is no more or less relevant than the many others suggested. Suffice it to say that after the end in France there was a slight reduction in aerial activity, as the Luftwaffe sought to recover from its not inconsiderable losses and establish new bases near the Channel coast. Many units were sent back to Germany to rest and recuperate, and consequently operations against Britain did not really start in earnest until early July.

Right:
Hurricane I L1607 of No 111 Squadron refuelling at Drem during an open day for the press, February/March 1940. A Spitfire of No 609 Squadron can be seen in the background. Units based at Drem, near Edinburgh, were involved in convoy patrols and the defence of naval vessels in the Firth of Forth. The Hurricane has the split black and white underside paint scheme, introduced before the war as a means of quick identification for anti-aircraft gunners and the Observer Corps. **HU 86065**

Below:
Also at Drem, this well secured Spitfire of No 609 Squadron has just fired a burst from three of its eight .303in Brownings into the butts. The ground below the port wing is littered with spent cartridge cases and belt links. A reporter appears keen to take a closer look as the ground crew prepare an encore. No 609 claimed its first success against a real target on 27 February when it shot down a Heinkel He111 off St Abbs Head. **HU 86064**

Above:
No 64 Squadron began the war as a night-fighter unit, equipped with
Blenheim IFs. In March 1940, when this photograph was taken, it was operating
at Church Fenton in the day-fighter role and had just taken delivery of its first
Spitfires. The 1,030hp Rolls-Royce Merlin III engine, visible here, gave the
Spitfire I a top speed (with emergency boost) of just over 360mph at 19,000ft.
It could climb quickly to height, but its radius of action was less than 200 miles.
HU 86062

There followed a month or so of probing attacks on ports and
Channel convoys as the Germans tested the British defences and
tried to entice the RAF into a battle of attrition. The attacks on
the convoys were of particular concern. Dowding was forced to
choose between losing fighters in defence of the ships or
husbanding his resources and allowing the strikes to be carried
out unmolested. He decided to commit only a fraction of his
force, and refused to allow his Command to be drawn into big
battles with the German fighters. This initial phase of the battle
saw a number of fierce engagements, which reached a peak on
8 August when seven ships from convoy CW9 were sunk off the
Isle of Wight, and 13 RAF fighters and 11 pilots were lost. In the
end, the losses in shipping proved unsustainable, and convoy
movements in daylight were halted.

By August Hitler had confirmed his intention of invading
Britain, and preparations were made for *Adlerangriff* ('Attack of
the Eagles'), an all-out air offensive during which the RAF
would be destroyed in the air and on the ground in preparation
for a cross-Channel assault. The Luftwaffe, its losses made good
and morale high after its recent successes, was numerically
superior, with some 1,200 bombers and 1,100 fighters ready for
operations in France and Belgium. A much smaller force of
about 160 aircraft was based in Norway and Denmark. By
comparison, the four groups of Fighter Command (No 10
Group had been recently created to defend the West of England)
had a total of 29 Hurricane and 18 Spitfire squadrons between
them, amounting to about 650 serviceable aircraft and 1,100
available pilots. In view of their geographical position, the 19
single-seat fighter squadrons of No 11 Group, under the expert
control of Air Vice-Marshal Park, would once again bear the
brunt of the fighting, although units would be rotated from
other parts of Fighter Command as the battle progressed. The
RAF's ace card was radar, and the fighter-control system that was
built around it. Avoiding the need to maintain wasteful standing
patrols, sufficient warning of incoming enemy formations would
be received for squadrons to be scrambled in time to meet and
engage them. It would prove decisive.

After successive postponements due to the weather, the
opening of the main assault, *Adlertag* ('Eagle Day'), took place
in the afternoon of 13 August when the Luftwaffe flew almost
1,500 sorties against airfields and other targets in southern
England. Faulty intelligence, however, massively reduced the
value of these attacks. The Luftwaffe bombed several aerodromes
unconnected with Fighter Command, believing them to be key
fighter bases. Inaccurate intelligence appraisals would continue
to bedevil German operations, as would the lack of any cogent
target strategy. Göring had issued his commanders with long

lists of objectives, including airfields, aircraft factories, shipping and ports, but without assigning any clear priorities to them. The mechanics of exactly how the RAF would be defeated had been given little thought either, save for a naïve belief that the Luftwaffe had merely to appear over England for the British fighters obligingly to rise and be shot down in large numbers. Most crucially of all, the Germans never fully appreciated the centralised nature of Fighter Command's command and control system, and displayed an astonishing degree of ambivalence towards the vulnerable RDF stations. After some early dive-bombing attacks that inflicted only temporary damage, attempts to destroy them were abandoned and the RAF's vital radar chain was left alone.

On 15 August the Luftwaffe launched its biggest operation yet, with RAF airfields as the primary targets. For the first time the bomber force based in Norway and Denmark was committed to the assault, but took such heavy losses (22 aircraft) that the attempt was never repeated. The Germans were more successful in the south, but still incurred serious casualties, bringing the total for the day to 70, their worst of the battle. On 18 August, in another major attack, the Luftwaffe lost a further 67 aircraft. In the face of such stiff resistance the bombers had to be massively escorted, and the Messerschmitts — which preferred to hunt on their own — were ordered to keep close to their charges. This decision rendered the German fighters far more vulnerable to the defending British aircraft, and was bitterly resented. Encounters with the RAF also quickly revealed fatal deficiencies in Luftwaffe equipment. The once feared Junkers Ju87 'Stuka' dive-bombers proved to be appallingly vulnerable — nine were shot down or written off on 16 August and a further 14 lost two days later. As a result they were quickly withdrawn from the battle. The Messerschmitt Me110 had also turned out to be a disappointment. Although fast and heavily armed, this twin-engined 'escort fighter' did not have the acceleration or manoeuvrability to prevail against Spitfires and Hurricanes.

The Me109s, superior at altitude and able to dive faster than the British fighters, were always the greatest threat and, although their effectiveness was somewhat reduced by their limited operational

Above:
Hurricane I L1951 of No 504 Squadron, part of a detachment based at Wattisham, came to grief during a combat with Heinkel He115 seaplanes off Great Yarmouth on 2 April 1940. Flying Officer David Phillips was wounded in the leg by return fire, and had to crash-land his aircraft. He was later credited with the destruction of one of the enemy machines. **HU 69945**

range, they exacted a heavy toll. By now the dangers of maintaining rigid formations were beginning to sink in, but most RAF squadrons were still flying in sections of three aircraft, albeit more thinly spread and with 'weavers' guarding the rear. Unfortunately the 'weavers' were often the first to be picked off. A few squadron commanders had begun copying the superior tactics of the Luftwaffe fighter arm, with aircraft operating in sections of four, but this would not become official practice until after the battle. As for the aircraft themselves, the RAF machines had few vices. The Spitfire was definitely a match for the Me109, the Hurricane less so, but the eight rifle-calibre machine-guns fitted to both types were not best suited to knocking down German bombers, which proved capable of absorbing considerable punishment. This led to some units experimenting with frontal attacks on the enemy formations, in order to hit the more vulnerable cockpit areas of the Heinkels and Dorniers, and avoid the deadly crossfire from their rear gunners.

In the last week of August and the first week of September the Luftwaffe intensified its attacks on No 11 Group's airfields, especially those around London. The strategically vital aircraft factories were also targeted. This was the most intensive and critical phase of the battle, when key sector stations such as Kenley, Biggin Hill, Hornchurch and North Weald were all subjected to heavy attacks. Luftwaffe losses remained high, but the RAF was suffering too, and pilot wastage had become Dowding's most pressing concern. Fighter Command lost 172 aircrew killed or missing in August alone, with many others wounded and out of action for varying periods. Thanks to increased factory production and the sterling efforts of the Civilian Repair Organisation, aircraft losses could be made good

extremely quickly, but the shortage of fliers was not so easily rectified. Operational training had been cut to the bone, which meant that replacements were turning up with only the minimum number of flying hours on Spitfires or Hurricanes. Many would perish without ever having got to grips with flying a high-performance aircraft, let alone the realities of air combat. A high proportion of experienced squadron and flight commanders had already been lost, so that many of those now leading the formations lacked combat experience. In desperation, other commands were 'combed' for suitable pilots, and use was made of the various volunteers from the Allied nations, most notably the Poles and Czechs who formed four squadrons in the later stages of the battle.

For pilots who survived long enough, the strain of combat and constant fatigue was beginning to take its toll. Where possible, 'burnt-out' units were sent north to rest and refit, but inexperienced squadrons brought in to replace them had little idea of what to expect, and were versed only in the RAF's traditional — but inadequate — fighter tactics. As the attrition continued, Dowding was forced to break up some of his squadrons in Nos 12 and 13 Groups, poaching their most experienced pilots to keep Park's No 11 Group going, and employing the rest to provide some further, much-needed training for the new intakes. This move was unpopular, but was better than committing whole new squadrons to the fighting which might suffer catastrophic casualties before they could usefully contribute. Experience counted for everything, but it was in short supply. The physical and mental exhaustion of a dwindling band of veterans was reducing Fighter Command's effectiveness more than anything else. The ground crews, too, were performing Herculean tasks, keeping shot-up aircraft airworthy and airfields open, sometimes in the face of bombing and strafing attacks. Understandably, some of them were cracking under the strain. It was a testing time, and Fighter Command was being stretched to the limit.

Throughout the battle both sides exaggerated their claims for enemy aircraft shot down, and the Germans consistently laboured under the misapprehension that they were making serious inroads into Fighter Command's resources. It is therefore ironic that in early September, when No 11 Group was beginning to suffer real harm, Göring should change the Luftwaffe's priorities and order mass daylight attacks against London. During the afternoon of 7 September over 900 German aircraft — two-thirds of them fighters — made straight for the capital and inflicted considerable damage, especially on the docks and the East End. This decisive shift in strategy has long been ascribed to Hitler's desire to avenge recent RAF raids on Berlin, but it was also intended finally to force a decision by attacking a target that would have to be defended in strength. The Germans hoped that hitting London would weaken Britain's will to continue the struggle, and in the process destroy what remained of Fighter Command. The immediate effect, however, was to take the pressure off No 11 Group's airfields and give Park's squadrons the breathing space they so desperately needed.

In the furious air combats of this period, the pilots of No 11 Group invariably found themselves outnumbered by the enemy. Air Vice-Marshal Park routinely sent only one or two squadrons in at a time, with the objective of breaking up the German formations as early as possible and disrupting their attacks — where possible, Hurricanes were directed at the bombers, and Spitfires at their escorts. He was careful to conserve his force, keeping other units at readiness to deal with subsequent raids. To protect his sector airfields while their resident squadrons were engaged, Park relied heavily on neighbouring groups for support. Air Vice-Marshal Sir Quintin Brand's No 10 Group co-operated faultlessly, but his opposite number in No 12 Group, Air Vice-Marshal Trafford Leigh-Mallory, was less willing to play a subordinate role. Fiercely opposed to Park's

Below:
Sir Samuel Hoare, the new Secretary of State for Air, inspects No 604 Squadron at Northolt, 6 April 1940. The squadron was a specialist night-fighting unit, operating Blenheim IFs, but months of patrolling had so far proved fruitless. In May the squadron at last saw action when it carried out daylight strafing attacks against German transport aircraft in the Netherlands. Its first aerial victory was a Heinkel He115 seaplane, shot down on 18 June.
HU 86060

'penny packet' approach, Leigh-Mallory sanctioned a tactic suggested by one of his squadron commanders, Douglas Bader. Already something of a legend in Fighter Command, Bader advocated a wing of three (later five) squadrons, based at Duxford, which would form up together and then engage the enemy in strength.

The so-called 'Big Wing' flew its first operational patrol on 7 September, but its subsequent deployment and effectiveness engendered considerable disagreement between Park and Leigh-Mallory. Assembling three or more squadrons inevitably took time, and on occasions Park's airfields north of London were left dangerously exposed. Often the German bombers were not intercepted until after they had bombed their targets and were heading for home. To some observers this was unimportant, as long as German aircraft were being shot down in large numbers. In fact, the Big Wing's claims were widely exaggerated and its squadrons flew together only five times during September. The controversy surrounding it, and the clash between Park and Leigh-Mallory, has long been overstated. Hitting the enemy in strength made sense as long as sufficient reserves were held back to deal with follow-up waves. What mattered most, though, was that the German formations continued to be engaged. By simply remaining in being, Fighter Command was denying the enemy control of the air, and winning the battle.

London remained the focus of the Luftwaffe's efforts during the first half of September, but if the Germans were expecting a lessening in resistance at this stage of the battle they were to be cruelly disappointed. Despite reassurances from their senior commanders that British reserves were virtually exhausted, the bomber crews continued to be intercepted in strength, not least by Bader's Duxford Wing. The appearance of RAF squadrons *en masse* undoubtedly had a demoralising effect. The effectiveness of the Luftwaffe's own fighters was also much reduced, thanks to steadily rising losses, and the fact that the Me109s were now having to operate at the very limit of their range. Increasingly, the RAF fighters were able to separate the enemy bombers from their escorts, with devastating results. On 15 September, regarded by many as the climax of the battle, there were two major actions, during which 28 RAF squadrons (approximately 270 Spitfires and Hurricanes) were involved. They destroyed 56 of the attackers for the loss of only 28 aircraft and 13 pilots.

A psychological turning point had been reached; Fighter Command sensed it had turned the corner, and the dispirited Luftwaffe finally realised it was not going to wrest air superiority from the RAF. Operation 'Sealion', the proposed invasion of

Britain, had already been put back several times, and now Hitler finally decided to postpone it indefinitely. Attacks continued for the rest of the month, mainly against aircraft factories, but the raiders often failed to reach their targets in the face of large numbers of British fighters. The outdated Heinkels and Dorniers, and even the newer and faster Junkers Ju88s, could not hope to operate in these conditions and were gradually switched to night operations. In October, with the weather deteriorating, the Luftwaffe reverted to fighter sweeps, and to entice the RAF up to defend its airspace some of the Messerschmitts were fitted with bomb racks. These fast and high-flying fighter-bombers (*Jagdbombers* or '*Jabos*') proved tricky to intercept, and imposed a severe strain on Fighter Command. Fortunately the strategic value of their attacks, many directed almost indiscriminately, was negligible. RAF losses were still high (140 aircraft and 84 pilots were lost on operations in October), but the intensity of the fighting was lessening.

The Luftwaffe had been carrying out sporadic night attacks over Britain since June, and these were now intensified following the failure of its daylight offensive. The German bombers could now only operate under the cover of darkness, and in the autumn and winter of 1940 they were launched against London and other major industrial centres. This new aerial offensive, which became known to the British as the 'Blitz', would impose on RAF Fighter Command an entirely new set of problems. As was the case with the other combatants, comparatively little attention had been paid to night-fighting in the prewar period, but Dowding had taken an active interest in experiments with airborne interception (AI) radar. By the middle of 1940 these had developed sufficiently for some primitive sets to be fitted into Blenheim IF fighters, the only aircraft considered suitable for the job. The early equipment proved to be temperamental, however, and the Blenheims themselves lacked the speed to catch fleeing enemy bombers. Most of the few kills that were achieved during the summer nights fell to single-seat fighters using searchlight beams and pot luck to make visual interceptions. AI had its first success on the night of 22/23 July when a Blenheim of the trials and experimental Fighter Interception Unit (FIU) managed to locate and shoot down a Dornier off the Sussex coast (a feat that would not be repeated for several months!). In September, when the German night attacks began in earnest, the six Blenheim squadrons available for night defence had only a handful of radar-equipped aircraft between them. Not only were most sorties fruitless, but also a lack of proper training in night flying meant that accidents were commonplace.

The entry into service of better radar equipment (AI Mk IV) and the superior Bristol Beaufighter held out hope of an improvement in Fighter Command's fortunes in the night war over Britain. Unlike the Blenheims, all the 'Beaus' were equipped with radar, and the sturdy new aircraft benefited from a good turn of speed and heavy armament. Beaufighters were delivered to four squadrons in September, but it was not until 19 November that Flight Lieutenant John Cunningham of No 604 Squadron achieved the type's first kill when he destroyed a Ju88. Most night sorties were still being flown by Blenheims,

Defiants and Hurricanes, and aerial victories were few and far between. On the night of the infamous raid on Coventry (14/15 November) 119 sorties were carried out against the Luftwaffe, but not a single enemy aircraft was shot down. It was a frustrating time, but the foundations were being laid for an effective night defence system. As the Blitz continued, Fighter Command's success rate would gradually improve.

At the end of November, Air Marshal Sir William Sholto Douglas replaced Dowding as C-in-C of Fighter Command. Dowding's departure — and that of his most able lieutenant, Air Vice-Marshal Park, who was also moved on — has long been criticised. The manner of their going, abrupt and without fanfare, still rankles with many veterans, and public recognition for both men's achievements was not forthcoming for many years. Their shabby treatment was motivated largely by the personal grievances of others, notably Leigh-Mallory, who now took over No 11 Group. Park found later fame when he expertly orchestrated the air defence of Malta, but Dowding, who was due to retire anyway, disappeared into oblivion. Both men have since been rehabilitated as the true architects of the RAF's most famous victory, but the whole episode remains a sad indictment on the political machinations of a number of individuals at the highest level.

Fighter Command's new chief now faced a different challenge. Although there was no reason to believe that the Luftwaffe would not renew its daylight onslaught in the New Year, for which Fighter Command would need to be prepared, the decision had already been taken to start hitting back at the enemy. In December Blenheim squadrons began 'intruder' operations over enemy airfields on the French coast, seeking to ambush enemy bombers returning from raids against Britain. By day, pairs of Spitfires began slipping across the Channel in conditions of low cloud and poor visibility, to shoot up targets of opportunity. These actions were the precursors of a new policy of 'leaning forward' into enemy-occupied Europe, an aggressive role which would involve the evolution of new tactics, new weapons and a new spirit. After a momentous year as Britain's shield, Fighter Command was poised to go on the offensive.

Opposite top:
Under a threatening sky, ground crew assist a Spitfire of No 72 Squadron taxiing from its dispersal at Acklington, April 1940. One man is weighting the tail down, which was standard practice on rough grass strips to prevent the propeller from striking the ground. The squadron had been based in the North since the outbreak of war, with convoy protection its main task. In June it moved south to help cover the Dunkirk evacuation. **HU 86061**

Opposite:
No 73 Squadron Hurricanes stage a mock 'No 1 Attack' on a Fairey Battle over France, 19 April 1940. In this manœuvre, a succession of single aircraft would line up and attack from astern, only breaking off when their ammunition was exhausted or the target destroyed. The RAF's 1938 *Manual of Air Tactics* was aimed solely at combating enemy bombers, preferably ones that flew straight and level and took no evasive action. Air combat between fighters was deemed impracticable due to the high speeds involved! Events had already undermined this fallacy, but Fighter Command's rigid and obsolete tactical doctrines could not be changed overnight, and would be responsible for many losses to come. **C 1288**

Right:
In late April 1940 No 263 Squadron was operating in freezing conditions from Lake Lesjaskog in Norway. A succession of Luftwaffe attacks on the 25th left 12 of its Gladiators wrecked, and the others were destroyed or abandoned in the days that followed. One of them, N5576, is seen here in June, long after the snow and ice had melted. The aircraft was later removed for preservation by the Norwegians.
HU 33715

Below:
No 73 Squadron pilots Sergeant Lionel Pilkington, Flight Lieutenant Reginald 'Unlucky' Lovett and Flying Officer Newell 'Fanny' Orton, April 1940. Lovett acquired his nickname as a result of a number of unfortunate mishaps, the most serious in December 1939 when he mistakenly shot down a French Potez bomber. Orton had recently claimed his fifth victory to become the RAF's second ace of the war. Lovett was killed during the Battle of Britain, while Pilkington (who was later commissioned) and Orton, serving with different squadrons, would die within days of each other in September 1941.
C 1329

Above:
Ground staff work quickly to prepare a Hurricane of No 73 Squadron for its next sortie, 12/13 May 1940. The aircraft has already been refuelled and armourers are replenishing its eight machine-guns. Each gun was fed with a belt of 333 rounds, sufficient for approximately 14 seconds' firing. The fuselage panel that has been removed gave access to the battery, oxygen bottles and radio equipment. **C 1546**

Left:
Once the *Blitzkrieg* had begun, the Hurricane squadrons in France were plunged into almost constant action, flying interception patrols and providing escort for RAF light bombers. Their airfields were subject to frequent Luftwaffe strafing attacks, with little or no warning. Here, personnel of No 85 Squadron at Lille-Seclin check air activity overhead while in the background two Hurricanes sit at 'stand-by', their pilots strapped in ready for immediate take-off, 10-12 May 1940. **C 1521**

Right:
Lewis gun at the ready, an airman watches for enemy aircraft from the cab of one of No 615 Squadron's lorries, 17 May 1940. Like the BEF, the RAF in France was well supplied with motor vehicles, but the frequent changes of location in the face of the enemy advance caused problems for the ground echelons. As the situation worsened, transport was often commandeered for other purposes and the carriage of fuel, ammunition and other stores was affected. **C 1607**

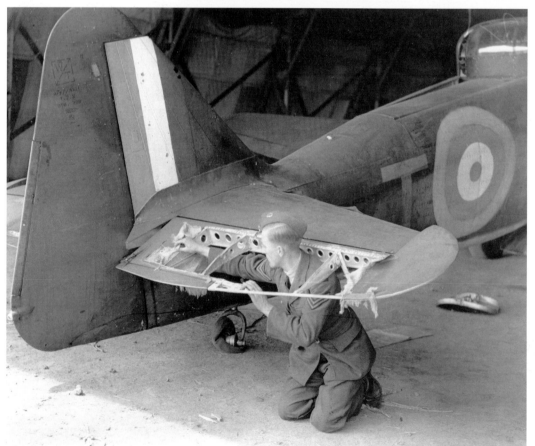

Left:
No 264 Squadron's Defiants first saw action on Channel patrols in mid-May 1940. Committed to the air battle over Dunkirk at the end of the month, the turret fighters' enthusiastic victory claims against enemy bombers belied their true effectiveness. Luftwaffe fighters quickly got the measure of the Defiant's unusual configuration, and losses were heavy. The photograph shows damage inflicted on L6957/PS-T, which limped back to Manston on 29 May minus its gunner, who baled out and was killed. **CH 184**

Above: Ready to go! The pilot of a No 501 Squadron Hurricane warms up his engine as helmeted ground staff disconnect the power supply from the 'trolley acc' (trolley accumulator). The photograph was taken at the end of May 1940, probably at Anglure, one of the temporary airstrips near Troyes to where the three remaining Hurricane squadrons in France had retreated by this date. The photographer noted that No 501 Squadron's unofficial score, after only a fortnight's activity, was 45 enemy aircraft destroyed. **C 1682**

Left:
German troops pick over the remains of a Spitfire, uncovered at low tide on the beach at Dunkirk, 4 or 5 June 1940. During the period of the evacuation — between 26 May and 3 June — Fighter Command lost 49 Spitfires. A similar number of Hurricanes also failed to return. The pilots of some of these aircraft were rescued after they baled out or crash-landed within the Dunkirk perimeter. **HU 83539**

Right:
Flying Officer John Allen of No 54 Squadron receives the DFC from the King at Hornchurch, 27 June 1940. Air Chief Marshal Sir Hugh Dowding stands in the centre, hands clasped behind his back. A month earlier, Allen had participated in the daring rescue of No 74 Squadron's CO from Calais-Marck airfield, helping to beat off enemy fighters while a two-seat trainer flew in to extricate the downed pilot. Allen claimed several victories during the Dunkirk evacuation, but was killed in action on 24 July. **CH 442**

Above: With canopy hoods slid back and flaps down, Spitfires of No 610 Squadron land over the western end of 'The Bump', as Biggin Hill airfield, perched on top of the North Downs, was known, July 1940. The ground falls away sharply behind the hedge on the right, which is why the third aircraft appears to be flying into rather than over it! The squadron was heavily involved in the battles over the Channel convoys at this time. **HU 87412**

Opposite top:
One of seven Junkers Ju88s brought down during attacks on airfields in Yorkshire on 15 August 1940. Spitfires of No 616 Squadron and Hurricanes of No 73 Squadron intercepted the enemy formation as it approached the coast near Scarborough. The Bomber Command airfield at Driffield was hit and nine Whitleys destroyed, but no RAF fighters were lost. Attacks further north, and in the South, were also repulsed at great cost to the Germans, on a day the Luftwaffe christened 'Black Thursday'. **HU 63859**

Opposite:
An RNVR officer of the Medway River Patrol inspects the wreckage of a Spitfire that came down on mudflats in early September 1940. Although not positively identified, the aircraft may have been a No 66 Squadron machine, shot down by Me109s over the Medway on 5 September. Pilot Officer P. King baled out but his parachute failed to open. **A 704**

Above:
Ground staff re-arm Spitfire I R6800/LZ-N, flown by No 66 Squadron's CO, Squadron Leader Rupert Leigh, Gravesend, 18 September 1940. Each ammunition box held a belt of 300 rounds, enough for one gun. By feeding the belts through the breeches using a length of webbing, the armourers were able to complete the whole process from below the wing. Not having to remove the upper wing panels reduced the time taken to re-arm the aircraft to less than 10 minutes. **HU 59066**

Above:
An official photographer took the following sequence of photographs during a visit to No 19 Squadron at Fowlmere, the satellite airfield of Duxford, in late September 1940. Here, a Spitfire of No 616 Squadron is given the 'once over' between sorties. From 19 September this squadron — normally based at Kirton-in-Lindsey — spent a month flying down daily to Fowlmere, to operate alongside No 19 Squadron as part of the 'Big Wing'. **CH 1359**

Left:
No luck this time. Sergeant Bernard 'Jimmy' Jennings of No 19 Squadron rests on a starter trolley while giving a combat report to the squadron 'spy' (intelligence officer). Jennings shot down an Me110 on 11 September and an Me109 at the end of the month, to add to his two previous kills over Dunkirk. He was commissioned in December and spent the middle war years instructing before returning to operations in 1944. **CH 1360**

Right:
Togged up. Flight Lieutenant Walter 'Farmer' Lawson, one of No 19 Squadron's flight commanders, shows off his flying kit. As well as his 'Mae West', he wears a Type B flying helmet, Mk II goggles and a Type D constant-flow oxygen mask. Lawson took over command of the squadron in July 1941, by which time he had shot down six enemy aircraft. He was killed in action the following month. **CH 1361**

Below:
Flying Officer Frank Brinsden, a New Zealander with No 19 Squadron, at ease in the spartan living accommodation at Fowlmere. Brinsden had been shot down on 31 August, but baled out safely. He went on to serve with three other squadrons, eventually becoming a Mosquito night-fighter pilot. In August 1943 he was forced to ditch his aircraft off the enemy coast, and spent the rest of the war in a prison camp. **CH 1466**

Right:
Spitfire I X4179/QV-B of No 19 Squadron. On 15 September this aircraft was used by Flight Sergeant George Unwin to shoot down two Me109s. X4179 survived its time with No 19 Squadron and went on to serve with several other operational units. It ended its days with No 57 Operational Training Unit (OTU), in whose hands it was written off in October 1943. **CH 1447**

Right:
They also served. RAF, WAAF and civilian clerks at work in the orderly room at Duxford, late September 1940. Gas-masks and helmets hang close by, but neither Duxford nor its satellite at Fowlmere was ever singled out for attack by the Luftwaffe. The only bombs to fall on or near them during the Battle of Britain were those jettisoned from fleeing German aircraft.
CH 1388

Below:
Flying Officer Hugh Tamblyn of No 242 Squadron, photographed on Squadron Leader Douglas Bader's Hurricane at Duxford, late September 1940. The predominantly Canadian-manned No 242 was one of three Hurricane squadrons in the Duxford Wing, led by Bader. Tamblyn had previously flown Defiants before joining his new squadron. He claimed five victories during the height of the Battle of Britain, and remained with the squadron until his death on operations in April 1941. **CH 1410**

Above: Workers from a Spitfire factory inspect one of their products in service, Mk II P7289 of No 266 Squadron at Wittering, October 1940. Such visits — and reciprocal tours of the factories by aircrew — continued throughout the war as part of the morale-boosting effort. The Spitfire II had only recently entered service; a more powerful engine gave it an improved rate of climb and service ceiling, but top speed was slightly down on the Mk I. **E(MoS) 1**

Left:
An RAF sergeant introduces two Czech fitters to the inner workings of a No 310 Squadron Hurricane at Duxford, October 1940. Formed from refugee Czech pilots and ground staff, the squadron had become operational in August as part of the Duxford Wing. Clearly visible in this photograph is the reserve fuel tank immediately in front of the cockpit, which was the cause of terrible cockpit fires if ignited during combat.
CH 1433

Above:

No 85 Squadron Hurricanes in flight, October 1940. After intensive action with No 11 Group, the squadron was now based at Church Fenton in Yorkshire, preparing for a new night-fighting role. The official establishment of a fighter squadron was 26 pilots and 16 aircraft (plus three or four in reserve), but numbers fluctuated considerably, especially during periods of heavy fighting. In late 1940 the average actual strength was 21 pilots. Squadrons usually operated with 12 aircraft, divided into two flights of six. **CH 1499**

Left:

In the summer of 1940 the first Polish squadrons were formed in Fighter Command. Many of their pilots were already combat veterans from the Polish and French campaigns. Despite language difficulties, the courage and tenacity of the Poles became legendary. No 303 'City of Warsaw' Squadron was the top-scoring RAF unit in September 1940, with nine of its pilots claiming five or more kills. Pilot Officers Jan Zumbach (left) and Miroslaw Feric were two of its aces. The photograph was taken at Leconfield in October, after the unit had retired north to recuperate. **CH 1537**

Above: Hurricanes of No 615 'County of Surrey' Squadron, Auxiliary Air Force, Northolt, 30 November 1940. The AAF had been set up in the mid-1920s on a territorial basis, each squadron staffed by part-time 'weekend fliers' (of the required social standing) drawn from the local area. The squadrons were absorbed into the regular Air Force before the outbreak of war, after which their prewar identity was gradually diluted by the influx of pilots from all over the country. **GSA 366-27**

Above: New shapes in the sky. Westland Whirlwinds of No 263 Squadron, December 1940. The Whirlwind's development had been protracted and secretive, but the result was a promising aircraft, as fast as a Spitfire at low level and heavily armed with four 20mm cannon. However, its Rolls-Royce Peregrine engines gave trouble from the start and frustrated further development. No 263 Squadron, based at Exeter, was the first of only two squadrons to equip with the type. **CH 4999**

1941

> *'The extravagance of an offensive which kept at most some two or three hundred German fighter pilots from joining their comrades on the Eastern Front or in the Mediterranean theatre was partly hidden by enormously exaggerated estimates of German losses.'*
>
> **(Official History, HMSO, 1957)**

In January 1941 Fighter Command comprised 70 operational squadrons, organised into six groups, and was about to undergo a massive expansion as more pilots and aircraft became available. The Hawker Hurricane remained the most prolific aircraft type in service, equipping no fewer than 39 squadrons, while Spitfires were on strength with 18. The Mk II versions of both types (outwardly similar but with more powerful engines) were now entering service with many units. Of the rest, five squadrons were operating Defiants, three were equipped with Blenheims and three more were flying the new Beaufighter. This last group, with some of the Hurricane squadrons, was busily engaged on night defence duties as the RAF struggled to counter the Luftwaffe's continuing Blitz on London and other cities. Meanwhile two new aircraft had entered service: the Havoc was a modified version of the American twin-engined Douglas DB-7 light bomber, employed in the night-fighting and intruder role; the Westland Whirlwind was a single-seat, twin-engined day fighter whose entry into service had been delayed repeatedly by technical problems. Neither aircraft would prove to be particularly successful.

Although Fighter Command was set to take the war to the enemy, its main priority in the first months of the year was the Luftwaffe's night bombing campaign. The Blitz had been raging since September 1940, but so far the British defences had enjoyed only minimal success against the enemy. The handful of kills that had been achieved were mostly the work of day fighters searching for the German bombers by the light of the moon or by the fires and searchlights of their targets. The Hurricane, more robust than the Spitfire and with a wide-track undercarriage, was better suited for night take-offs and landings, and a number of squadrons had been officially converted for this role. The two-seat Defiant, having proved such a failure in daylight, was enjoying something of a revival as a night-fighter. If manoeuvred with skill, its four-gun turret could blast an enemy bomber from below, but the aircraft was still far from ideal. A more radical experiment was the Turbinlite, a version of the Havoc, fitted with a powerful nose-mounted searchlight with which it tried to illuminate enemy bombers for accompanying Hurricanes to shoot down. Eventually most Havocs would be converted for this role, but despite the input of a considerable amount of time and effort the Turbinlite project was a dismal failure. The future lay with the radar-equipped and powerfully armed Beaufighters that were now beginning to enter service in some numbers, and which would eventually swing the balance in favour of the defenders.

Successful night interceptions depended not only on the effectiveness of airborne radar and the abilities of the crews but also on the skills of the ground controllers. By January the first six GCI (Ground Control of Interception) installations had become operational, covering the southeastern approaches to London and the Midlands. These provided operators with a radar map of the action, with fixes on both hunter and hunted. In concert with IFF (Identification Friend or Foe) equipment in the RAF aircraft, which enabled the radar plotters to separate friendly 'blips' from those of the intruders, and a chain of radio beacons to help pilots navigate over blacked-out Britain, the GCI stations could direct a night-fighter to within two or three miles of an enemy aircraft. After that the interception would continue using the AI set aboard the aircraft itself, until the target was finally picked up visually. (Fighters without radar were also controlled in this way, their pilots of course totally dependent on the 'Mk 1 eyeball' to make a contact.) As winter gave way to spring, this system contributed to an astonishing rise in the number of enemy bombers destroyed. In March 1941, when six Beaufighter squadrons were operational, 22 bombers were confirmed destroyed, and another 48 were claimed in April. In May almost 100 enemy aircraft were shot down by night fighters of all types. After many months of frustration, Fighter Command was at last beginning to win the night battle over Britain.

By day Luftwaffe fighter-bombers continued to probe the British defences, and Fighter Command was forced to maintain defensive patrols in the hope of catching the fast-moving raiders. Convoy protection in coastal waters constituted another important if unglamorous element of its workload. Of more significance for the future, however, was the beginning of Fighter Command's own offensive against the Luftwaffe over enemy-occupied Europe. The simplest type of operation was called a 'Rhubarb', in which small numbers of aircraft — often just a pair — used bad weather to penetrate enemy airspace at low level and strafe any targets that appeared. Rhubarbs became a routine activity for Fighter Command squadrons in the front line, but flak and the marginal conditions in which the sorties were flown resulted in a level of attrition that far outweighed the damage inflicted on the enemy.

Larger forces comprising several squadrons flew fighter sweeps at high altitude in the hope of engaging the Luftwaffe, but the Germans were under no obligation to challenge these incursions. As the RAF had found during the Battle of Britain, enemy fighters on their own posed little threat and could be safely ignored. Something was needed to entice the German fighters into the air. The result was the first 'Circus' operation, flown on 10 January, which involved 11 fighter squadrons accompanied by six Blenheim bombers from No 2 Group, Bomber Command. The Blenheims' target was an ammunition store at an airfield near Calais, but their primary role was to act as bait for the Luftwaffe. In the event the German response was limited, and only one Me109 was claimed by the RAF, for the loss of two of its own fighters.

Circuses and fighter sweeps continued throughout the spring, but had little effect on the Luftwaffe and proved costly for the RAF. In the first five months of the year 51 pilots were killed in action or taken prisoner. In that time it is estimated that barely 20 enemy fighters were destroyed, although many more were claimed. The RAF squadrons now faced all the problems that had beset the German fighters over Britain during the previous year. Operations had to be conducted over enemy territory, with two crossings of the Channel to contend with. Range was the great limiting factor — neither the Spitfire nor the Hurricane could penetrate further than about 60 or 70 miles inland from the enemy coast at its closest point (roughly as far as Lille). Flying flat-out in hostile airspace — necessary for survival, especially on the low-level Rhubarbs — burned up fuel at an accelerated rate. On Circuses, fighters flying close escort to the bombers were vulnerable to the 'bounce', and depended for protection on other squadrons positioned above them. The Luftwaffe fighters were able to climb higher still, and enjoyed the luxury of being able to decide when and where to attack. Alerted by radar, the enemy pilots would position themselves 'up sun' of the British, diving down to strike at the most opportune moment, and any RAF pilots who survived being shot down were invariably captured.

The aircraft destined to carry the burden of Fighter Command's offensive was the Spitfire, production of which increased dramatically during 1941. The number of Spitfire squadrons rose from 18 to 46 by the end of the year, as new units were formed and existing ones converted. Operations with the Mk I and Mk II had revealed the need for better altitude performance and a heavier cannon armament, resulting in the new Mk V, essentially a re-engined and up-gunned Mk I. Although only intended as a stop-gap pending the development of the Mk III (which in the end never materialised), the Spitfire V became the most numerous version of this classic fighter. No 92 Squadron at Manston received the first aircraft in February, and by June six squadrons had converted to the type. In the quest for range, attempts were made to increase the Spitfire's fuel capacity by fitting non-jettisonable auxiliary tanks to the port wings of a number of Mk IIs. These asymmetric 'long-range' Spitfires made their debut in June, but proved such a handful in combat that their use was restricted mainly to escorting bombers on coastal shipping strikes (codenamed 'Roadsteads') where enemy fighters were less likely to appear.

In contrast to the Spitfire, the Hurricane was lagging behind as a pure fighter, especially at altitude, and was gradually being replaced by its faster and more agile stablemate in this role. In the spring, versions of the Hurricane II appeared with 12-gun (Mk IIB) or four-cannon armament (Mk IIC), but useful though this increase in fire-power was, in terms of performance the aircraft was no match for the Luftwaffe's latest fighter, the

Below:
The Hurricane of Squadron Leader Robert Stanford Tuck, commanding No 257 Squadron, refuelling at Coltishall, early January 1941. Bob Tuck was a crack shot and one of Fighter Command's leading aces, with 19 confirmed kills at this time. His aircraft, V6864/DT-A, has an 18in-wide 'sky blue' band painted around the rear fuselage, which together with a similarly coloured spinner had recently been introduced as a recognition marking for all RAF day fighters.
CH 1931

Me109F. The Hurricane squadrons continued to take part in offensive operations, but were increasingly relegated to anti-shipping and ground-attack duties, usually with Spitfires acting as 'top cover'. The Hurricane's replacement, the Typhoon, was in the final stages of development, but, owing to a host of problems with its powerplant, would not reach the squadrons until the autumn. That other new type, the Westland Whirlwind, had also begun operations on a limited scale with No 263 Squadron, mainly on convoy escorts over the Channel. Later it too would be adapted for the fighter-bomber role.

Fighter Command's escort operations and sweeps were becoming increasingly sophisticated, requiring careful planning, good organisation and improved tactics. The role of the RAF ground controllers was growing in importance, and the range and accuracy of radar reporting over Europe improving. The controllers were responsible for directing the air battle, monitoring the progress of friendly squadrons and relaying information on the height and direction of hostile forces. In the air, large wing formations of three or more squadrons, identified by the sector station around which they were based, now acted in concert, and much depended on the 'wing leaders' who commanded them. One of the first and most inspirational was Wing Commander A. G. 'Sailor' Malan, a South African who led the Biggin Hill Wing. His 'Ten Commandments' of air fighting were eventually disseminated throughout Fighter Command. Pilots were urged to make use of height, keep a constant lookout and turn to meet enemy attacks — diving

away invariably spelled disaster, as the enemy fighters had the edge on speed. As always, only a minority of pilots mastered the art of 'deflection shooting' — knowing instinctively how far ahead of a turning fighter to aim to secure a fatal hit; they also knew the importance of getting in as close as possible before opening fire. These men became the aces; most pilots would struggle — and ultimately fail — to emulate them.

By now squadrons were experimenting with a variety of tactical formations, as they sought to improve on the outdated and vulnerable 'vics of three'. Malan was again the principal innovator, dividing his own unit into three sections of four aircraft, so that in battle each would break down into two fighting pairs, as practised by the Germans. This formation — flexible, cohesive and mutually supporting — was a vast improvement on what had gone before and was soon being employed by other squadrons. In most units the four-aircraft sections flew in line astern, which was easy to fly and afforded security to the aircraft in front, but was less safe for those pilots last in line. The famed legless ace Douglas Bader, leading the Tangmere Wing, preferred a line-abreast battle formation, the so-called 'finger-four', which more closely mirrored the

Below:
Many hands make light work. In a scene rather too obviously set up for the camera, the pilot of a No 249 Squadron Hurricane looks on as his aircraft is re-armed, North Weald, 28 February 1941. No 249 participated in some of the earliest Rhubarb and Circus operations over enemy territory. In May, the squadron left Fighter Command for Malta, converted to Spitfires and spent the rest of the war in the Mediterranean and southern Europe. **CH 2530**

Luftwaffe's *Schwarm*. Here there were no vulnerable positions in the formation, as all aircraft could cover each other's tails. It proved a great success and ultimately became standard RAF practice for the rest of the war.

On 22 June 1941 Hitler's armies invaded the Soviet Union, an event that had major repercussions for Fighter Command. The night Blitz had suddenly tailed off in May as the German bomber fleets were moved east. Now, with most of the Luftwaffe engaged in this enterprise, the RAF was given fresh impetus to increase the pressure and tie down as many enemy aircraft as possible in the West. Fighter Command was ordered to step up its range of offensive actions during what became known as the 'summer offensive'. During this intensive period, Circuses, Rhubarbs and sweeps were carried out almost continuously. There were some 90 escorted raids, mostly against easily reached targets between Lille and Rouen, and hundreds more fighter sweeps and strikes against harbours and shipping along the Channel coast. When the weather clamped down, individual aircraft sought targets of opportunity on low-level Rhubarbs.

Although much was made publicly of Fighter Command's aggressive role, the actual results of the upsurge in activity were disappointing. The Germans had seen fit to leave only two single-engined fighter wings in northern France (JG 2 and JG 26), which never numbered more than about 200 aircraft in total, but proved more than capable of dealing with the RAF incursions. British losses increased dramatically. In the four months from June to September Fighter Command lost approximately 300 pilots over enemy territory. The casualties included some of its most experienced commanders: on 25 June the Hornchurch wing leader, Wing Commander Joe Kayll, was shot down and captured; on 9 August Douglas Bader also baled out into captivity; and Wing Commander John Gillan, leading the North Weald Wing, was killed during a sweep on 29 August.

If the RAF was learning valuable tactical lessons, the Luftwaffe continued to enjoy advantages in equipment. The Me109F and Spitfire V were very closely matched, but the German fighter had a superior operational ceiling and rate of dive. In the confusion of battle, RAF pilots continually mistook the puff of black smoke emitted from its Daimler-Benz engine when diving away at full power as evidence of a hit, which was one reason for the wildly exaggerated claims that characterised fighter operations during this period. In September the balance was swung further in the Luftwaffe's favour with the appearance of a new fighter, the Focke-Wulf FW190. This fast, radial-engined aircraft exceeded the performance of the Spitfire V in almost all areas, and was far superior to any other RAF type. Like many new aircraft, the Focke-Wulf had its share of teething problems, but by the end of the year about 100 had been delivered to units in France.

A new type of operation instigated in late 1941 was the 'Ramrod', in which bombers were escorted to strike at specific targets, the destruction of which was now the primary aim. Bomb-carrying Hurricanes found a niche role in low-level fighter Ramrods against shipping and ground installations along the enemy coast. No 607 Squadron initiated the first of these 'Hurribomber' sorties on 30 October, attacking an electricity transformer station, and No 402 Squadron bombed an airfield two days later. The Whirlwind, now in service with two squadrons, was also pressed into action against ground targets, its formidable armament particularly useful for strafing airfields and shipping. Such targets were heavily defended, and light flak claimed many victims on these dangerous 'deck-level' sorties. But it was the FW190 that posed the greatest threat to the continuation of the RAF's daylight offensive. Circuses were suspended for a month after a disastrous operation to Lille on 8 November when nine RAF fighters and seven pilots were lost (the casualties including a wing commander and three squadron leaders). Eleven more pilots were lost on other sorties that day. The Air Ministry ordered Sholto Douglas to curtail all but the most essential operations. The 'non-stop

offensive' would continue, but on a greatly reduced scale, mostly in the form of Rhubarbs and attacks on coastal targets, where the danger from enemy fighters was much reduced.

After a year of sustained fighter-versus-fighter combat on the fringes of Europe, Fighter Command had emerged distinctly second-best to the Luftwaffe. The RAF had lost 560 fighters on daylight offensive operations, almost two-thirds of them during the summer 'shooting season'; another 200 or so had been lost on defensive scrambles, patrols or night sorties. The Germans, whose own losses from all causes were barely a quarter of this combined figure, had never felt the need to divert forces from Russia to deal with the RAF's challenge. But despite its casualties, and the increasing number of units being sent to bolster Britain's ailing fortunes in the Middle East, the healthy supply of aircraft and new pilots was such that Fighter Command was able to expand to 100 squadrons by the end of 1941. Pressure remained on Sholto Douglas to increase his Command's contribution to the defence of coastal shipping, and he could not rule out the possibility of a resumption of massed Luftwaffe daylight attacks in the New Year. However, at a time when Britain was still very much on the defensive, Fighter Command's offensive over Europe represented one of the few ways of striking back at the enemy. Whatever its efficacy, it would remain a key part of the RAF's strategy for some time to come.

Below:
'Eagle' Squadron. American pilots of No 71 Squadron rush to their Hurricanes at Kirton-in-Lindsey, 17 March 1941. Formed in September 1940, No 71 was the first of three squadrons of volunteers from the United States to be established in Fighter Command (Nos 121 and 133 Squadrons became operational later in the year). All were amalgamated into the USAAF in September 1942. **CH 2401**

Above: The Duke of Kent talks to ground staff carrying out checks on a Hurricane II of No 601 'County of London' Squadron, during a visit to Northolt on 19 March 1941. Cleaning brush and rag in hand, a fitter explains the various maintenance routines that have to be carried out on the aircraft's 1,280hp Merlin XX engine. **CH 2291**

Right:
A No 264 Squadron Defiant ready to begin a nocturnal patrol from Biggin Hill on the night of 9/10 April 1941. Seven squadrons of Defiants were involved on night defence duties at this time, and five more formed later in the year. Few claims were made against the German bombers, however. During the summer, small numbers of radar-equipped versions of the aircraft began entering service, but were nowhere near as effective as other night-fighters. **CH 2520**

Above: The pin-up painted (or glued?) on the side of this Hurricane attracted the attention of a photographer at Drem on 25 April 1941. Unfortunately the image was deemed by higher authority to be unfit for publication and duly censored. 'Wee Jean' was an aircraft from No 260 Squadron, a recently formed unit that was about to leave Fighter Command for the Mediterranean. **H 9195**

Above:
Spitfire VBs of No 92 Squadron, May 1941. The first cannon-armed Spitfires (Mk IBs) saw action with No 19 Squadron during the Battle of Britain, but had to be withdrawn from service due to constant ammunition stoppages. With the problem solved, the 'B' wing armament of two 20mm cannon and four .303in machine-guns became standard on nearly all Mk Vs. No 92 Squadron operated from Biggin Hill during the spring and summer of 1941, taking part in offensive sweeps, bomber escorts and Rhubarbs.
CH 2931

Left:
A pilot demonstrates the new 'K'-type one-man dinghy in the unlikely surroundings of Watford Public Baths, 19 May 1941. Experience had shown that while the standard 'Mae West' could keep a man afloat, it could not stop him succumbing to hypothermia after only an hour or so in the freezing waters of the Channel or North Sea. The new dinghy, introduced in early 1941, enabled fighter pilots who baled out over water to survive for many hours — or even days — when they might otherwise have perished before rescue could arrive.
CH 2851

Left:
A study in concentration. Pilot Officer James 'Ginger' Lacey DFM and Bar, hard at work in No 501 Squadron's dispersal hut at Colerne, 30 May 1941. Lacey, recently commissioned, had been with the squadron since 1939, and had become famous as the top-scoring pilot of the Battle of Britain. At the time of this photograph his personal score stood at 23 confirmed kills and five 'probables'. **CH 2814**

Right:
An RAF 'ground gunner' mans a 20mm Hispano cannon in a revetment at Tangmere, 8 June 1941. Coastal airfields remained vulnerable to Luftwaffe 'hit-and-run' attacks. To supplement the Bofors guns deployed by the Army at such locations, RAF airfield defence flights had been formed, equipped with a variety of automatic weapons. In 1942 these were amalgamated into a new organisation, the RAF Regiment, dedicated to protecting bases at home and abroad. Note the Blenheim night-fighter of No 219 Squadron in the background. **CH 4624**

Above:
Spitfire IIs of No 65 'East India' Squadron at Kirton-in-Lindsey, 18 June 1941. Based at Kirton for much of the year, the squadron undertook convoy patrols over the Channel, and later flew sweeps and bomber escorts during the 'summer offensive'. The two aircraft closest to the camera, P8136/ YT-V and P8147/ YT-W, survived service with a succession of operational squadrons, OTUs and the Central Gunnery School. Both were struck off charge in November 1944.
CH 2922

Left:
Also photographed at Kirton on 18 June were these pilots of No 452 Squadron, the first in Fighter Command to be composed almost exclusively of Australian personnel. Formed in April 1941, the squadron spent a working-up period at Kirton before transferring to Kenley to begin operations on cross-Channel sweeps. In June 1942 the unit shipped out to take part in the defence of Australia. **CH 2883**

Above: One of the few photographs to show bombers and their escorting fighters together. Hurricanes of No 312 Squadron fly close escort to a Stirling bomber, one of three acting as bait during Circus No 33 to Lille on 5 July 1941. As was now routine on these complex operations, several squadrons of Spitfires would be flying at various altitudes above as escort cover, high cover and top cover. Other wings provided support over the target and withdrawal cover as the force made its way home. **C 2028**

Above: High-scoring pilots of No 611 Squadron at Hornchurch, 7 July 1941. From left to right: Flight Lieutenant Eric Lock, Pilot Officer Wilfred Duncan-Smith, Flying Officer Peter Dexter and Sergeant William Gilmour. Lock was a Battle of Britain veteran with 24 confirmed kills. He was posted missing on 3 August after strafing ground targets. Dexter, too, was killed, only a week after this photograph was taken, when he collided with another Spitfire on a bomber escort. Both Duncan-Smith and 'Mac' Gilmour survived, finishing the war with 17 and nine confirmed victories respectively. **CH 3056**

Above: Yeomen of England. No 91 Squadron Spitfire pilots at the butts, Hawkinge, 23 July 1941. Archery was in vogue with several squadrons, a supplement to the more usual forms of recreational target practice. Such images were also used by the Ministry of Information to promote the idea that all fighter pilots were marksmen. No 91 Squadron was employed on various tasks at the time, including coastal reconnaissance patrols (known as 'Jim Crows'), Rhubarbs and Air-Sea Rescue escorts. **CH 3319**

Above:
Spitfire pilots of No 234 Squadron relax at Warmwell, 26 July 1941. Note the ubiquitous Lloyd Loom basket chairs, and walls festooned with a mixture of trophies, pin-ups and instructional posters of enemy aircraft. Since its formation in October 1939 the squadron had spent much of its time in the West Country, and was currently flying convoy patrols and bomber escorts to the French ports. **CH 3430**

Opposite:
The Prime Minister of New Zealand, The Rt Hon Peter Frazer, climbs from the cockpit of a No 92 Squadron Spitfire VB at Biggin Hill on the evening of 11 July 1941, during his whistle-stop tour of South Eastern Command. The visit was not allowed to interfere with operations, which were intensive during this period. No 92 Squadron had already lost six aircraft and four pilots since the beginning of the month. **H 11650**

Above: Newly built Beaufighter IF X7583 on 1 August 1941, during a press visit to Bristol's assembly plant at Old Mixon, near Weston-super-Mare. It was the first time the Beaufighter had been revealed to journalists. The aircraft had established itself as the most potent night-fighter in the world, with a maximum speed of over 300mph, ample space to accommodate its bulky radar equipment and a powerful armament of four 20mm cannon and six machine-guns. This particular aircraft was delivered to No 68 Squadron. **HU 56560**

Above: As part of the war effort, private individuals and organisations were encouraged to donate money towards the cost of a new aircraft, an example of which would then be marked with an appropriate acknowledgement and 'presented' to the RAF. Spitfire II P8448 was funded by NAAFI canteen workers and bore the name *Counter Attack*. It is seen here being officially handed over to No 152 Squadron at Portreath on 8 August 1941 by 19-year-old Nora Margaret Fish. This Spitfire was one of the few 'long-range' Mk IIs fitted with a fixed 40gal fuel tank under the port wing. The asymmetric arrangement impaired the aircraft's flying characteristics and was not successful. **CH 3614**

Above: A superb view of No 3 Squadron Hurricane IICs, based at Hunsdon, 2 September 1941. Four 20mm cannon gave the Mk IIC a hefty punch, but the relatively slow Hurricane was now restricted to low-level sweeps, Rhubarbs and anti-shipping operations. To mask further the aircraft's shortcomings, squadrons were turning increasingly to night or dusk operations. Detachments from No 3 Squadron had just begun flying intruder sorties from Shoreham and Manston. **CH 3498**

Above: Hurricane IIBs of Duxford-based No 601 Squadron blend into the patchwork of fields below, 21 August 1941. RAF day-fighter camouflage was changing to reflect the fact that operations were now being conducted at higher altitudes, and routinely involved flights over water. Ocean grey and dark green uppersurfaces had replaced the dark earth and dark green of 1940. Undersurfaces were now medium sea grey. Sky spinners and tail bands were retained, and yellow outer-wing leading edges also added for identification purposes. **CH 3518**

Above: No 485 Squadron was the first of three New Zealand squadrons in Fighter Command, becoming operational in April 1941 and taking part in operations over France during the summer. These are Spitfire VBs at Redhill, a satellite airfield to Biggin Hill, on 26 September 1941. All the aircraft were funded by various gift schemes in New Zealand; the aircraft in the foreground is W3528, donated by the Women's Division of the Farmers' Union of New Zealand, while in the background can be seen the CO's mount, AB870/DU-Z *Hawkes Bay I*. **CH 3751**

Left:
With panels removed, the armament of a Hurricane IIB (Z3661 of No 3 Squadron) is revealed. Each wing held six .303in Browning machine-guns, four in the main bay and two in the outer wing; 3,990 rounds of ammunition were normally carried. 'Hurribombers' often had a pair of the inboard guns removed to allow space for the bomb racks, in which case over 5,000 rounds could be stowed. The photograph was taken at Hunsdon on 6 September 1941.
CH 3522

Above:
A Hurricane IIB of No 79 Squadron refuelling at Fairwood Common, Swansea, September 1941. The pair of 44gal external fuel tanks doubled the aircraft's range to 935 miles. No 79 saw little action during 1941, being engaged mainly on convoy patrols and the defence of South Wales and the Midlands. In March 1942 the squadron was transferred to India. **HU 86315**

Right:
Flight Lieutenants Brendan 'Paddy' Finucane (left) and Keith 'Bluey' Truscott of the Australian No 452 Squadron congratulate each other at Kenley on 13 October 1941. The two flight commanders had just returned from a very successful Circus operation during which each had shot down two Me109s. Dublin-born Finucane was shot down and killed by ground fire in July 1942, having destroyed over 30 enemy aircraft. Truscott lost his life while serving in New Guinea in March 1943. **CH 3759**

Left:
No 601 Squadron parade their new Bell Airacobras for the press at Duxford, 17 October 1941. The squadron's relationship with this unconventional American fighter was a brief and unsuccessful one. Inadequate performance, servicing difficulties and a host of accidents resulted in the Airacobra being rejected by the RAF. No 601 used the type operationally on only four occasions, and was happy to re-equip with Spitfires in the spring of 1942. **HU 48128**

Right:
Clipped wings. A Luftwaffe NCO notes the identity of Spitfire VB W3824/ DV-F, now resident in a salvage yard somewhere in northern France, 28 November 1941. The No 129 Squadron aircraft was shot down on 27 September 1941 during Circus No 103. Its pilot was captured. The operation had been typically costly — in addition to W3824 nine other RAF aircraft failed to return. **HU 86316**

Above: The forgotten night-fighter — a radar-equipped Havoc II, photographed in October 1941. This variant had a formidable battery of 12 machine-guns mounted in the nose. More might have been made of the Havoc, but only No 85 Squadron employed the aircraft in the conventional night-fighting role, operating Mk Is and Mk IIs between April 1941 and September 1942. Almost all the RAF's Havocs were eventually converted into Turbinlite searchlight carriers. **HU 2154**

Above: A No 402 Squadron 'Hurribomber' being re-armed at Manston, 6 November 1941. The pair of 250lb bombs were dropped from very low level, usually against heavily defended targets such as airfields and ships. Despite attempts by cannon-armed Hurricanes to suppress the flak, losses were heavy — especially on the hazardous 'Channel Stop' anti-shipping operations. No 402 flew relatively few 'Hurribomber' sorties, unlike No 607 Squadron — also based at Manston — which lost 10 aircraft in November and December. **CH 3901**

Left:
No 1 Squadron's CO, Squadron Leader James MacLachlan, in the cockpit of his Hurricane IIC at Tangmere, 20 November 1941. 'Mac' MacLachlan began his RAF career flying Fairey Battle bombers during the Battle of France. After transferring to fighters he served on Malta, but lost his left forearm — shattered by a cannon shell — in February 1941. Despite his disability he resumed flying duties in the UK, becoming an outstanding night intruder pilot. Later attached to the Air Fighting Development Unit, he was killed over France in July 1943 while flying a Mustang. **CH 4014**

Below:
Sergeant Eugeniusz Nowakiewicz of No 302 Squadron adopts a classic Churchillian pose on the wing of his Spitfire at Exeter, November 1941. Nowakiewicz was one of the 130 refugee Polish pilots who, before coming to Britain to join the RAF, fought with the French Air Force during the Battle of France. He scored three individual and two shared kills to become the top-scoring Polish pilot of that campaign. In 1942 he was shot down over Europe, hidden by the Resistance and captured by the Gestapo, but survived the war. **HU 86383**

Air Marshal Sir William Sholto Douglas, C-in-C Fighter Command, with Flight Lieutenant Brian Kingcome during a visit to No 61 OTU at Heston, November 1941. Kingcome, a Battle of Britain veteran and eight-kill ace, was serving as an instructor at the unit — a normal 'rest' activity for pilots taking a break from operational flying. He later returned to the sharp end, spending the latter half of the war in the Mediterranean. **CH 4209**

Below:
One of the first Mosquito II night-fighters, seen after a demonstration flight during a visit by the Duke of Kent to the de Havilland plant at Hatfield in November 1941. The nose-mounted transmitter aerial and wing-mounted receiver aerials for the aircraft's AI Mk IV radar are visible. The Mosquito II had a top speed of 380mph and entered operational service with No 157 Squadron in the spring of 1942. **E(MoS) 516**

Above: 'Evelyn', a No 23 Squadron Havoc 'fighter-bomber', starts up at Ford at the beginning of another night sortie, 28 November 1941. The squadron's Havocs retained their original glazed nose compartments, were armed with four forward-firing machine-guns and carried a crew of three. They often carried a light bomb load as well, and were used exclusively for intruder operations against enemy bomber bases. **CH 4048**

Above: Aircraft and ground staff of 'B' Flight, No 253 'Hyderabad' Squadron, at Hibaldstow, 23 December 1941. The Hurricane IIBs are in overall black finish, befitting their nocturnal defence role at this time. All aircraft were funded by contributions from the Indian State of Hyderabad. Z3971/SW-S *Samasthans II*, in the foreground, was one of many Hurricanes later given to the Russians, but was lost at sea *en route*. **CH 4391**

Above:
Spitfire VB AA879 *Manchester Civil Defender* of No 616 Squadron, pictured during a press visit to Kirton-in-Lindsey in December 1941. In accordance with standard Fighter Command practice, the squadron had been temporarily withdrawn from the front line after a hectic summer of offensive operations with the Tangmere Wing. Its time in winter quarters was spent on training flights, air-firing exercises and convoy patrols. **HU 66616**

Right:
The only Australian night-fighter squadron in Fighter Command, No 456 was formed in June 1941 at Valley in North Wales. The photograph shows armourers relaxing in their quarters in December of that year. They are, from left: Doug Andrews, Archie Clarke, Fred Howe, George Bryan and Herb Eacott. The message on the door reads: 'Please mind your language. Don't forget there are WAAFs about!' **CH 4632**

The war situation looked decidedly bleak for Britain in the early part of 1942. In North Africa British forces were locked in a seesaw struggle with Rommel, as they sought to defend Egypt and the Suez Canal. The beleaguered island fortress of Malta, thorn in the side of the Axis supply routes to the Afrika Korps, was in desperate need of fighters to fend off Italian and German air attacks. Further afield, the Japanese were sweeping all before them in the Far East, and German U-boats were continuing to take a huge toll of merchant shipping in the North Atlantic. With the Russians battling the vast bulk of Hitler's armies, pressure was building on Britain for greater action in the West, but a cross-Channel invasion was clearly a long way off. Only the RAF was able to take the war to the enemy, though the results were as yet far from commensurate with the effort expended. Bomber Command was struggling with an increasingly costly — and largely ineffective — night bombing campaign over Germany, while Fighter Command, after a year of heavy losses, was conceding the daylight battle for superiority over the Luftwaffe.

Despite the consternation caused by the appearance of the FW190, Air Marshal Sholto Douglas had no option but to press on with the offensive over northwest Europe. The force at his disposal had expanded numerically, but was facing a crisis in terms of equipment. The Hawker Hurricane, serving with 13 squadrons, was now fit only for night-fighting and ground-attack work, while its replacement, the Typhoon, was beset with problems and only just operational with two units. The burden would continue to be shouldered by the Spitfire V squadrons, of which a total of 35 were operational in Nos 10, 11 and 12 Groups, with another 19 squadrons located further north.

The first major operation of 1942 occurred on 11 February when the Germans instigated a daring plan to sail three of their capital ships — the battle-cruisers *Scharnhorst* and *Gneisenau*, and the heavy cruiser *Prinz Eugen* — from the French port of Brest back to home waters. They chose the shortest and most dangerous route for the breakout — the English Channel — but this enabled the ships and their escorting destroyers to be covered by a massive umbrella of Luftwaffe fighters. Aware of the possibility of such a move, the British had a contingency plan in place (codenamed 'Fuller'), which involved RAF bomber, torpedo and fighter squadrons, as well as units from the Royal Navy and Fleet Air Arm. However, stifling secrecy, poor communications and a general lack of co-ordination between the various commands meant that the German vessels were already passing through the Straits of Dover before the alarm was raised. In the frantic actions that followed, 18 aircraft of Fighter Command were lost, either to flak or in dogfights with the numerous escorting fighters (including many FW190s). The heroic air and surface attacks on the German ships themselves came to nought.

After this set-piece, Fighter Command resumed its staple fare of Circuses, Ramrods, Roadsteads and Rodeos (the last being the new name for large-scale fighter sweeps), but by now the qualitative superiority of the Luftwaffe was all too apparent. RAF losses were consistently high, with each operation often costing squadrons one or two aircraft, sometimes more: on 25 April No 501 Squadron lost five aircraft; on 9 May six aircraft were shot down after No 118 Squadron received a mauling from JG 26; on 2 June No 403 Squadron lost no fewer than eight Spitfires, although most of the pilots survived. Although the Me109 was still potent (the new 'G' model or 'Gustav' entered service in May), the FW190 reigned supreme and was now in widespread service. Approximately 280 RAF aircraft — mostly Spitfires — were lost in the first five months of 1942 on daylight sorties over enemy territory. This level of attrition could not continue, and in June the Air Staff once again instructed Sholto Douglas to limit operations to attacks on coastal targets only.

Fortunately for Fighter Command an answer to the Focke-Wulf menace was close at hand. Once again it was a stop-gap version of the Spitfire, already under development, that offered the most promise. In the previous autumn the manufacturer had married the powerful new Rolls-Royce Merlin 61 engine to some existing airframes, creating a new version of the aircraft, designated the Mk IX. Performance was vastly improved on the Mk V, especially at altitude, thanks to a two-stage supercharger and four-bladed propeller. The new aircraft was initially only intended as a temporary solution pending the arrival of the substantially redesigned Mk VIII, still in the development and testing stage, but would in fact be built in considerable numbers (eventually equipping a total of 90 RAF squadrons). No 64 Squadron at Hornchurch was fortunate enough to introduce the Spitfire IX into combat, receiving its first aircraft in early July. Fighter Command finally had an aircraft to match the FW190, and, although the German fighter was more manœuvrable and could still dive faster, the Spitfire had the edge on speed at most altitudes. On 30 July No 64 Squadron flew its first operation with the new 'Spits', shooting down three Focke-Wulfs for no loss.

With much of the Luftwaffe's bomber strength still committed to the Russian Front, there had been little pressure on Britain's night defences over the winter of 1941/2. However, destructive Bomber Command attacks on the Baltic ports of Lübeck and Rostock in March and April led Hitler to demand retaliation. The so-called *Baedeker* raids that followed (named after a 19th-century German guidebook for foreign travellers to Britain) were directed against some of Britain's historic and less well defended cities, including Bath, Canterbury, Norwich and York. Casualties were high and damage was extensive, but the Luftwaffe would pay a high price. In the year since the Blitz had ended, the RAF's night-fighter force had increased in size and capability. The Beaufighter was now the backbone of the force, equipping 14 squadrons. A few were fitted with new, short-wavelength 'centimetric' radar, designated AI Mk VIII. This high-powered device focused a fine beam of energy using a revolving dish reflector contained within a nose-mounted radome. Its minimum and maximum range, clarity and resistance to false echoes from the ground at low level were far superior to the earlier metre-wavelength AI Mk IV. Centimetric radar represented one of the major advances of the war, but for the purposes of security its use over enemy territory would be prohibited until June 1944.

The spring of 1942 also saw the introduction to operations of a new night-fighter, the de Havilland Mosquito II. The design of the twin-engined, all-wooden Mosquito had received a lukewarm response from the Air Ministry when first (privately) developed, but once the prototypes had demonstrated the aircraft's astonishing capabilities, orders were placed for reconnaissance, bomber and fighter versions. To say that the 'Mossie' went on to become one of the most versatile and successful aircraft of the war would be an understatement. Initially, the most urgent need was for a more effective night-fighter, and the Mosquito — fitted with AI Mk IV radar — was considered ideal for the role. Nos 151 and 157 Squadrons were the first to receive the new aircraft, flying their first operational sorties at the end of April. Despite a number of contacts, success proved elusive until the night of 29/30 May, when Squadron Leader G. Ashfield of No 157 Squadron claimed a 'probable' victory over a Dornier Do217 off Dover. On the same night, pilots from No 151 Squadron engaged a number of enemy bombers over the North Sea, though none was brought down. In June No 264 Squadron joined the fray, and over the following summer nights the Mosquito force exacted a small but steady toll of Luftwaffe bombers. By the end of September a dozen kills had been confirmed.

Below:
Pilots and Hurricanes of No 56 'Punjab' Squadron at Duxford, 2 January 1942. The official caption reads: 'Fighter aircraft donated by the Province of the Punjab have been in action and have scored numerous victories over the Hun.' In fact, the squadron achieved little success on night patrols over the winter months. It was more concerned with getting its new Typhoons operational, examples of which had been delivered the previous autumn. 'Punjab' has been chalked onto the black-painted aircraft for the benefit of the photographer. **CH 4547**

Above:
Fitters adopt industrious poses around the 1,030hp Rolls-Royce Merlin III
of a No 125 Squadron Defiant at Fairwood Common, January 1942.
The 'Newfoundland' Squadron was one of several new night-fighter units to
form during 1941. Unfortunately it had to wait until the end of April 1942 before
scoring its first kill, a Heinkel He111 shot down over Bath. The Defiants
remained in use until May, by which time the squadron had re-equipped with
Beaufighters. **CH 4607**

The Mosquito crews had an aircraft that was faster and lighter at the controls than the Beaufighter, possessed a greater range and was almost as heavily armed, with four 20mm cannon and four machine-guns. These qualities made it eminently suited to offensive night operations as well, and in July No 23 Squadron pioneered the first Mosquito intruder sorties over enemy airfields. Later in the year No 264 Squadron began flying night 'Rangers', seeking out enemy aircraft, trains and motor transport on freelance missions to wherever the crews felt there might be suitable targets. Mosquitos used in this way had their radar equipment removed and extra fuel tanks fitted, but supplies of aircraft were very limited at first as most were required to counter the *Baedeker* raids. The German attacks on Britain continued sporadically, and with decreasing effectiveness, until October, by which time the Luftwaffe had lost 40 bombers to RAF night-fighters.

Another new aircraft now finally in service was the Hawker Typhoon, successor to the Hurricane. First delivered to No 56 Squadron in September 1941, the Typhoon was dogged in its development and early career by problems with its powerful Napier Sabre engine, as well as structural failures and seepage of carbon monoxide into the cockpit. By August 1942, three squadrons (Nos 56, 266 and 609) had been formed into the Duxford Typhoon Wing, the first victory coming on the 9th of

that month when No 266 Squadron shot a Ju88 into the sea off the Norfolk coast. Several other units started re-equipping with Typhoons in the late summer. However, the performance of the new fighter came as something of a disappointment. Designed originally to carry six cannon for destroying bombers, the aircraft had a massively thick wing, a factor that effectively ruined its manœuvrability above 15,000ft. Fortunately it also possessed a top speed of almost 400mph at sea level, which meant it was the only aircraft in Fighter Command's inventory that could catch an FW190 'on the deck'. Until now the fast, bomb-carrying *Jabos* had been virtually invulnerable on their 'tip and run' raids against coastal targets. In September five Typhoon squadrons were redeployed to southern airfields, from where they mounted increasingly successful standing patrols against these raiders.

On 19 August 1942 Fighter Command fought its greatest air battle since the summer of 1940, in support of a large-scale combined-operations raid on the French port of Dieppe.

Above: 'B' Flight of No 409 Squadron, Fighter Command's first Canadian night-fighter unit, pose for a formal portrait with one of their Merlin-engined Beaufighter IIs at Acklington, January 1942. The squadron's English CO, Wing Commander D. G. Morris, is seated in the centre, flanked by the adjutant, the intelligence officer and the two flight commanders. The squadron had seen plenty of action defending Tyneside and the North East. Its score stood at five enemy bombers destroyed and several others damaged. **CH 4903**

Above: Winter weather brought its own problems, especially at the more northerly locations. After a heavy snowfall, pilots and ground staff alike were required to pitch in with shovels to keep the aircraft flying. This Spitfire of No 603 Squadron taxies out at Dyce for another routine convoy patrol, 4 February 1942. In the spring No 603 was split up and its aircraft and pilots despatched to Malta aboard the American carrier USS *Wasp*. **CH 4838**

Operation 'Jubilee' was intended to test the enemy defences and assess the feasibility of capturing and holding a port — an objective that might well feature in a future cross-Channel invasion. A force of 6,000 troops was involved, mainly Canadians, with tank and Royal Navy support. The air effort was immense, and was controlled by No 11 Group, which had been reinforced for the operation. Hurricanes, Whirlwinds and Typhoons braved the flak to attack enemy gun positions, transport and ground installations, while 48 squadrons of Spitfires (including four with Mk IXs) established a protective umbrella over the beachhead. The shield held, despite vigorous attempts by the Luftwaffe to get at the ships and troops below.

For a large number of the RAF combatants, Dieppe was their first taste of intensive action, and many returned claiming victories. The Air Staff had hoped to lure much of the Luftwaffe to destruction, but official figures of over 100 enemy aircraft destroyed, and many more damaged, were widely exaggerated. In reality, 48 Luftwaffe aircraft were shot down, of which only 23 were fighters. Fighter Command lost 100 aircraft and 52 pilots killed or captured. Fifteen more were wounded. The raid itself ended in failure. Unable to make any real progress, the troops were taken off after nine hours of fighting. Half their number had been killed, wounded or made prisoner. If any lessons for the future had been learned, they had come at a price.

Also in August 1942, a new component to Fighter Command's escort role was added when the United States Eighth Air Force began bombing operations from Britain. The four-engined B-17 Flying Fortresses and B-24 Liberators were heavily armed, and were expected to hold their own against enemy fighter opposition on daylight deep-penetration raids. The fallacy of this belief would soon be discovered, but for now the American 'heavies' restricted their attacks to targets in France and the Low Countries, during which Spitfires provided cover as far as their limited range would allow. Other squadrons mounted diversionary sweeps and ground-attack operations in support. The RAF's participation in these missions would continue, even after USAAF fighters became available in large numbers, but the lack of range which bedevilled most types of Allied single-seaters at this time, especially the Spitfire, would allow the Luftwaffe to engage the American bombers with impunity for well over another year.

Despite the failure of the *Baedeker* raids, the Luftwaffe's own bomber force was not entirely spent, and reopened its night bombing assault on a reduced scale in the autumn and winter months of 1942. The *Kampfgruppen* faced an unenviable task. The RAF had on its side the benefit of two years' experience, as well as continuing improvements in training and technological 'wizardry'. Successful interceptions were becoming routine, and the skies over Britain an extremely dangerous place for the German crews. Nor were they any safer over their own territory; lurking RAF intruders waited to strike at enemy bombers returning to their airfields in France and the Low Countries. Specialist Hurricane squadrons had been successfully engaged in this role for many months, as had those equipped with Havocs and Bostons. No 418 Squadron not only attacked airfields but utilised the bomb-carrying capability of its Boston IIIs to strike at small industrial targets as well. When caught in the open, railway locomotives also attracted the prowling RAF fighters, providing some consolation if no enemy aircraft were about. In November, the CO of No 609 Squadron, Roland Beamont, introduced the Typhoon to offensive night operations with some solo train-busting Rhubarbs over northern France. As already noted, the Mosquito was beginning to make its mark, and it was this aircraft above all others that would come to dominate the night skies on both sides of the Channel.

As the year closed, Fighter Command's broadening night intruder effort was becoming a key part of the RAF's offensive. By day, too, the spirit of attack continued to manifest itself through the costly Rhubarbs and low-level strikes against the enemy coast. Although the Typhoon appeared to hold some promise as a ground-attack aircraft, it was unfortunate that it had failed in the pure fighter role. Air superiority — still Fighter Command's prime function — continued to depend on the Spitfire; but again, it was a source of some concern that the Mk IX had merely matched (rather than dramatically overtaken) the performance of the FW190. Such was the soundness of the Spitfire's original design that it would stand further development, and versions with Rolls-Royce's new-generation Griffon engine were almost ready for service. However, it was the aircraft's lack of range that posed the greatest challenge, particularly now that Fighter Command's escort duties were expanding. It was hardly the fault of the designers; much of the blame lay with official decisions, taken much earlier, not to build a long-range fighter, on the grounds that such an aircraft could never compete with short-range interceptors. More than three years into the war, Fighter Command was still mostly geared for defensive operations, and lacked the means to project its strength deeper into enemy territory.

Below:
Working breakfast. Squadron Leader Charles Green, commanding 'A' Flight of No 600 Squadron at Predannack, checks up on the serviceability of his Beaufighters after a night of patrolling over the West Country, April 1942. Green was a former Spitfire pilot who, after recovering from a serious wound received over Dunkirk, was posted to night-fighters. He went on to command the squadron after it was transferred to North Africa later in the year. Note the rack of rifles and 'Tommy gun' ready for use behind. **CH 5428**

Right:
Hurricane IIC BD936/ZY-S of No 247 Squadron, April 1942. The squadron had been based in the South West since its formation in the summer of 1940, and in the spring and summer of 1942 alternated between Exeter and Predannack. Main activities were Rhubarbs, night intruders and anti-shipping operations, the last also usually carried out under the cover of darkness. The unit's all-black aircraft wore non-standard small fuselage roundels and codes, an early example of low-visibility markings. **CH 5486**

Below:
Spitfires of Nos 72 and 124 Squadrons stage a flypast over Biggin Hill during a visit by the King and Queen in April 1942. Both squadrons are split into the standard sections of four, with aircraft flying in line-astern formation. The Spitfire V in the foreground is BM370/ ON-W, recently delivered to No 124 Squadron. The censor has marked the gun pits on the left for removal before publication. **HU 87413**

Above: A Czech Spitfire pilot of No 313 Squadron in conversation with his rigger and fitter at Hornchurch, 8 April 1942. His aircraft is BL581 *Moesi-Ilir*, a Mk VB presented by the Netherlands East Indies Fund. No 313 was the third and last Czech fighter squadron to form in Fighter Command. Its spell at Hornchurch on sweeps, escorts and Rhubarbs in the spring of 1942 was costly — 12 aircraft and 10 pilots were lost in less than three months. **CH 17971**

Above:
A Spitfire VB of No 303 'City of Warsaw' Squadron at Northolt, 10 April 1942. The aircraft is having its cannon tested at the butts. The unit's famous 'Kosciuszko' badge has been painted under the windscreen, with the Polish Air Force national marking on the nose. Northolt was very much home to the Polish fighter squadrons in Britain. At the time of this photograph, the Northolt Wing comprised Nos 303, 316 and 317 Squadrons. **CH 5506**

Above: Flight Lieutenant J. E. 'Johnnie' Johnson, a flight commander with No 616 Squadron, smiles from his Spitfire VB at Kingscliffe, 13 April 1942. A protégé of Douglas Bader, Johnson had six confirmed kills. He had little opportunity to add to this total during 1942 (his next victory was an FW190 over Dieppe in August), but scored steadily thereafter. One of the great fighter leaders, he ended the war as the RAF's official top-scorer with 34 enemy aircraft — all of them fighters — to his credit. **HU 87763**

Above: A smart line-up of Spitfire Vs of No 91 'Nigeria' Squadron at Hawkinge, 5 May 1942. Squadron Leader 'Bobby' Oxspring stands nearest the camera with Mk VC AB216/ DL-Z *Nigeria: Oyo Province*. The Mk VC was fitted with the 'universal' or 'C' wing, which could accommodate four 20mm cannon or, as here, the more usual combination of two cannon and four machine-guns. **CH 5429**

Right:
'The story of a sweep.' The following five photographs are from a sequence taken on 7 May 1942 at Hornchurch, and later released by the Ministry of Information to illustrate a typical offensive operation (the original captions have been retained in inverted commas). In the first, 'a flight takes off, as seen from the control tower. The characteristic oval shape of the Spitfire wings is clearly seen in the ground shadows...'. Spitfires of No 122 Squadron get airborne. **CH 5761**

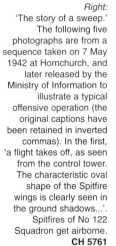

Left:
'The flight is up. A few minutes ago pilots sprawled at ease in these chairs. Already they are many miles away and climbing steadily...' The bicycle leaning against the dispersal hut and the dog waiting patiently for its master to return complete an evocative picture. **CH 5763**

Right:
'Fitters and riggers enjoy a well earned rest...' There was little for the ground staff to do once 'their' aircraft had departed on an operation. These members of No 122 Squadron while away the time with a game of draughts — using washers and circlips as playing pieces — as they wait for the Spitfires to return. **CH 5767**

Left:
'Pilots discuss experiences on the sweep they have just made. The squadron leader has apparently something interesting to tell...'
Squadron Leader Wilfred Duncan-Smith, commanding No 64 Squadron (back to camera, arm in the air), goes over the operation with his pilots and the squadron intelligence officer. He is wearing a Luftwaffe life-jacket. On 17 May he shot down an FW190, his eighth confirmed aerial victory.
CH 5780

Below:
'Immediately aircraft return from the sweep they are seized by ground crews and refuelled, rearmed, and checked over. The pilot's oxygen bottle, one of which is in the foreground, is renewed at once...' In the bright spring sunshine, a No 64 Squadron Spitfire VB is readied for another sortie.
CH 5772

Above: Flight Sergeant Georges Nadon of No 122 Squadron was the focus of another photo-story taken at Hornchurch in May 1942. This time, the photographer's brief was to record the movements of a single pilot over the course of a day. The 27-year-old French-Canadian, seen striking a pose in the cockpit of his Spitfire, was asked to list his hobbies. Somewhat predictably, the response was 'girlfriends and beer'! He survived the war after service on Malta and in northwest Europe.
CH 6781

Right:
Group Captain Charles Lott, Hornchurch's 35-year-old Station Commander, climbs into his flying kit before going up in a Spitfire, June 1942. Lott had lost an eye commanding No 43 Squadron in 1940, an injury that ended his operational career, but not his progress upwards in the RAF (he retired as an Air Vice-Marshal in 1959). Retrieving his parachute from the car is his WAAF driver, Leading Aircraftwoman Mary Ford. **CH 6817**

Right:
Wing Commander Ian 'Widge' Gleed in the cockpit of his Spitfire V, 16 June 1942. Gleed was leading the Ibsley Wing at the time, consisting of Nos 118, 234 and 501 Squadrons. His aircraft bears his initials ('IR-G') as identification letters, a privilege granted to those of wing commander rank and above. It also carries his famous 'Figaro the Cat' personal emblem, and a wing commander's pennant. Gleed was shot down and killed in the Mediterranean in April 1943. **CH 5908**

A year and a half after its introduction into service, the Spitfire VB was still Fighter Command's most numerous aircraft type, equipping 59 squadrons either operational or forming. These are aircraft of No 81 Squadron, part of the Hornchurch Wing, photographed in June 1942. In the autumn the squadron was taken out of the line and readied for service in North Africa. **CH 6381**

Right:
'Butcher-Bird'. The Focke-Wulf FW190A was arguably the best fighter aircraft in the world in the summer of 1942, but it was not invincible. This one's demise was captured by the gun camera of an attacking Spitfire over France in July. Another Spitfire can be seen in the background. The Focke-Wulf undoubtedly conferred a huge advantage on the Luftwaffe, but pilot skill, tactics and luck played an important part in the outcome of any engagement. **C 3007**

Above: The Brazilian Ambassador, Señor Moniz de Aragoa, greets Flight Sergeant A. Williams of No 111 Squadron during a presentation ceremony at Debden on 12 June 1942. Spitfire VB BM634, a gift from the State of São Paulo, was formally handed over to the squadron and christened *O Bandeirante* ('Flag Bearer'). The Ambassador is flanked by Treble One's CO, Squadron Leader P. Wickham (left), and the Station Commander, Group Captain J. R. Peel. **CH 5942**

Left:
After completing basic and advanced flying training, fledgling fighter pilots spent a further period at an OTU, where they were introduced to the aircraft they would fly in combat. Pilot Officer G. Walsh (right) is seen with his instructor after his first flight in a Spitfire at No 61 OTU at Rednal, August 1942. The number of Spitfire OTUs reached a peak of five in May 1942, but was reduced later in the war when losses did not reach predicted levels and pilots were required for other types. **CH 6454**

Above: In November 1941 the first squadron of Belgian volunteers was formed in Fighter Command. One of its pilots was Pilot Officer H. A. Picard, seen here on the wing of his Spitfire at Kenley in July 1942. His aircraft was among a number 'presented' by the Belgian Congo, and bears the name of one of its principal towns. Picard was shot down and captured on 27 August. Imprisoned in Stalag-Luft III at Sagan, he took part in the 'Great Escape' of March 1944, but was one of the 50 men subsequently rounded up and executed by the Gestapo. **CH 6356**

Above: Spitfire VBs of No 453 Squadron at Drem, 14 August 1942. Originally formed in Australia for service in Malaya, where it was destroyed by the Japanese advance, No 453 was reborn in Scotland in June 1942, again with Australian personnel. The Spitfires in the photograph still bear the codes of their previous owners, No 331 Squadron (No 453 was assigned 'FU'). After a working-up period on convoy patrols, No 453 Squadron flew south to participate in the cross-Channel offensive. **CH 6512**

Above: Sergeant B. Bawden of Sydney and Hurricane IIC HL865 *Night Duty*, both of No 87 Squadron at Charmy Down, 2 September 1942. The aircraft was one of two Hurricanes presented by members of the nursing profession (the other was christened *Nightingale*). After almost two years spent mainly on night defence and intruder operations, No 87 Squadron was about to leave Fighter Command for service in North Africa. **CH 6931**

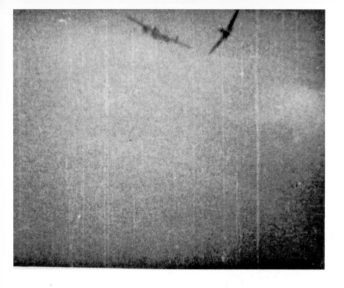
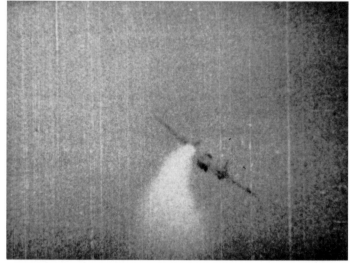
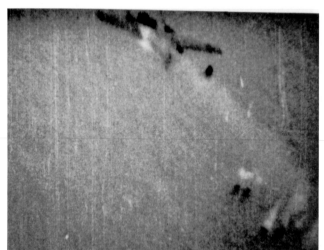
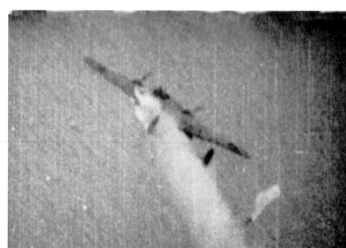

Above:
The last moments of a Dornier Do217 over Dieppe on 19 August 1942, as recorded by Sergeant Helge Sognnes of No 331 Squadron. A member of the bomber's crew can be seen escaping by parachute, moments before the aircraft plunged into the sea. Sognnes shared the kill — his first — with another Spitfire (visible in the first frame of the sequence). The Norwegian pilot went on to score steadily, shooting down five FW190s before being killed on a bomber escort over the Netherlands in June 1943. **C 3195**

Right:
Thanks, Navy! An RAF flight sergeant is hauled from the sea off Dieppe, 19 August 1942. During a day of intense aerial combat 61 pilots from Fighter and Army Co-operation Commands were killed or captured, but at least 20 more were rescued after baling out or ditching. Official Air Ministry statements declared a victory and claimed that the Germans had lost a quarter of their western fighter strength during the battle. In reality only 23 Luftwaffe fighters were lost, and 14 pilots killed. **FLM 1109**

Above: Fighter leaders. Group Captain Charles Appleton (centre), Station Commander at Tangmere, flanked by some of the wing leaders and squadron commanders who flew on the Dieppe Raid. On the left, Wing Commanders 'Johnnie' Walker (Tangmere Wing) and 'Pat' Gibbs (Ibsley Wing). On the right, Squadron Leaders 'Bertie' Wootten (No 118 Squadron) and 'Bobby' Yule (No 66 Squadron). Seated on the Hurricane behind is 'Dan' Du Vivier, the Belgian CO of No 43 Squadron. The photograph was taken on 20 August 1942. **HU 88314**

Right:
In September 1942 No 418 Squadron, RCAF, was operating Boston IIIs on night intruder sorties from Bradwell Bay. Its usual targets were Luftwaffe airfields, the French railway system and occasionally factory buildings. The aircraft in the photograph carry ventral fuselage gun packs housing four 20mm cannon. No 418 Squadron continued its nocturnal activities over the winter, converting to Mosquitos in the spring of 1943. **CH 7210**

Above: Spitfire LF VB BM271/SK-E *Kenya Daisy* of No 165 Squadron returns to its dispersal at Gravesend on 16 October 1942. The Spitfire's restricted view forward meant it was necessary for the ground crew to guide the pilot when taxiing, and hanging off the wingtips helped bring the aircraft to a halt! Introduced in the second half of 1942, the LF V had a modified engine (the supercharger impeller blades were 'cropped'), which produced a maximum speed of about 350mph at 6,000ft. As a result the aircraft was as fast as a Focke-Wulf at low altitude. **CH 7686**

Above:
Spitfire IX BS456/UZ-Z of No 306 Squadron, photographed at Northolt on 16 November 1942. The Mk IX was probably the most important variant of the famous fighter to see service. Thanks to its Merlin 61, with two-stage supercharger and intercooler, the new Spitfire had an extra 300hp on tap at 30,000ft compared with the Mk V. This particular aircraft was later transferred to No 316 Squadron, but was shot down by FW190s over the Channel on 22 August 1943. **HU 87411**

Left:
An engine fitter identified only as 'Lofty' featured in a series of official photographs taken at Middle Wallop in December 1942, intended to illustrate the vital but unsung daily activities of a typical 'erk' (as all junior RAF ground staff were known). Lofty is seen here with his charge, Spitfire VC EE624/TM-R, flown by Squadron Leader R. Lewis, commanding No 504 Squadron. **CH 8010**

1943

> *'How we longed for a wing of Spitfires which could fly to Berlin and back, for fighter pilots of every nationality were agreed that the Spitfire IX was the best close-in fighter of them all. But our radius of action remained the same as before, and we had to confine our activities to short-range operations…'*
>
> (Air Vice-Marshal J. E. 'Johnnie' Johnson CB, CBE, DSO and Two Bars, DFC and Bar)

In 1943 the war would swing decisively in the Allies' favour, with Germany under pressure on all fronts. As far as the British and Americans were concerned, most progress was being made in the Mediterranean. The successful conclusion of the campaign in North Africa was followed in the summer by landings in Sicily and Italy, as the assault on the 'soft underbelly' of Europe got underway. These unfolding events had ramifications for Fighter Command back in Britain, principally as a result of aircraft and personnel being despatched for service in these theatres. In the autumn of 1942, a dozen fighter squadrons had been diverted to North Africa to support Operation 'Torch', the Anglo-American landings in Algeria and Morocco. Six more squadrons were sent out early in the New Year. Units on the Mediterranean and southern European fronts, as well as those further afield in India and Burma, continued to demand fighter aircraft, especially the latest Spitfires, all of which reduced the resources available to Fighter Command at home.

Fighter Command was now led by the ambitious Air Marshal Trafford Leigh-Mallory, who had been appointed to replace Sholto Douglas in November 1942. Despite the drain of units already mentioned, the new Commander-in-Chief still had a sizeable force of 100 squadrons at his disposal. Much of their work would continue as before, the principal objective being to maintain pressure on the Luftwaffe in northern France and the Low Countries. Escort duties were the highest priority, and these would increase in scope and frequency as the RAF's day bombers, as well as the American medium and heavy bomber forces, stepped up their strategic and tactical bombing effort. Later in the year, with preparations for that ultimate Allied goal, the invasion of France, well underway, Fighter Command would undergo major organisational changes as many of its fighter and ground-attack elements were allocated to the support of that great undertaking.

Of the 47 Spitfire squadrons available at the beginning of 1943, only 10 were equipped with the Mk IX. Owing to difficulties producing enough engines, and demands for the aircraft from other battlefronts, it remained in short supply. This situation did not markedly improve until the second half of the year. As a result, the vast majority of home Spitfire units had to soldier on with the Mk V, even though this aircraft was in most respects totally outclassed by the opposition. In an effort to extend its useful life, many airframes were converted into LF Vs, with 'M' series Merlin engines rated for low-altitude performance and wing-tips removed ('clipped') to add a few more miles per hour. Useful though these modifications were, the Spitfire V had become a liability at higher altitudes, and wherever possible was restricted to the close escort of medium bomber formations.

The Spitfire IX was now available in three versions, of which the most important and by far the most numerous was the LF IX. This aircraft was fitted with the Merlin 66 engine, designed to give optimum performance at the altitudes at which the FW190 was most effective. Although the LF IX was officially designated a 'low-altitude fighter', the term was relative and its top speed of just over 400mph was actually attained at 21,000ft, compared to 25,000ft for the standard F IX fitted with the Merlin 61 or 63. A third and much less common variant, the HF IX with the Merlin 70, was geared for high-altitude work. The Spitfire IX had another advantage, as described by 'Johnnie' Johnson, when appointed to command the Kenley Wing: '…apart from its longer nose and more numerous exhaust stacks, it looked exactly like the inferior V. From the usual combat range it was impossible for the Luftwaffe pilots to distinguish between the two types, and this suited me, for I had a score or two to settle.'

Nos 124 and 616 Squadrons were equipped with the Spitfire VI, a specialised variant with a pressurised cockpit intended to combat high-altitude German raiders. Earlier in the war, lone Ju86 bombers had over-flown Britain on reconnaissance flights, including regular runs over the Home Fleet anchorage at Scapa Flow. These aircraft operated at well over 40,000ft, and had remained invulnerable despite many attempts by Fighter Command to catch them. From August 1941 nuisance bombing attacks had also been carried out, culminating in a raid on Bristol during which 48 people were killed. By the beginning of 1943 most of these sub-stratosphere incursions had petered out, but high-flying FW190 *Jabos* and Me109 reconnaissance aircraft remained a threat, prompting the retention of a number of specialist high-altitude units. Nos 124 and 616 Squadrons later received the Spitfire VII, another limited-production high-altitude interceptor. These were scrambled against the occasional intruder, but by now there were few calls on the high-flying Spitfires to perform in their intended role. Instead, both squadrons spent most of their time on sweeps, convoy patrols and providing top cover on escort operations, for which the increased internal fuel capacity of their aircraft proved useful.

Luftwaffe 'tip and run' fighter-bombers continued to tax Britain's defences in the first half of 1943, keeping the Typhoon squadrons busy over the Channel. The FW190s usually came across singly or in pairs, invariably in cloudy weather, keeping to wave-top height to avoid radar detection. On a number of

Above: Group Captain A. G. 'Sailor' Malan on the wing of Squadron Leader Hugo Armstrong's Spitfire IX at Biggin Hill, 2 January 1943. The South African had just taken command of the station, and was one of Fighter Command's most respected leaders. He was officially credited with 32 kills, all obtained during 1940 and the first half of 1941. 'Sinker' Armstrong, an Australian, led No 611 Squadron and had eight aerial victories. He would claim two more before being shot down and killed over the Channel in February. **CH 8108**

occasions they attacked in force — 28 aircraft penetrated as far as London on 20 January, but only 19 made good their escape. Eastbourne, Hastings, Lowestoft and Great Yarmouth were the targets of other notable raids, but the results of their efforts were inconsequential. No 609 Squadron was particularly successful during this period, and claimed 27 out of the 57 *Jabos* shot down between October 1942 and the middle of 1943. A new Spitfire variant, the Mk XII, had also been selected to join the battle against these 'sneak raiders'. It was powered by the new Rolls-Royce Griffon engine, optimised for performance at low altitude, and featured 'clipped' wings to further increase its speed and rate of roll. No 41 Squadron flew the first operational sorties in April, but the second unit to equip with the type, No 91 Squadron, enjoyed more success initially, claiming six FW190s attacking Folkestone on 25 May. The two squadrons were also involved in offensive sweeps over northern France.

On the night of 17 January the Luftwaffe carried out its first major raid on London since 1941. Sporadic night attacks against the British Isles continued throughout 1943, but the German bombers suffered heavy casualties from the RAF's increasingly expert night-fighter force. At the beginning of the year, seven Mosquito and 13 Beaufighter squadrons were operational, many of the latter now operating the improved Mk VIF version. Useful though it still was, the Beaufighter was gradually giving way to the far superior Mosquito, which was rapidly establishing itself as Fighter Command's principal defensive night-fighter. By the summer the number of Mosquito squadrons had grown to 10, many with the new Mk XII fitted with centimetric radar. Mosquitos achieved at least 80 confirmed kills over Britain during 1943 for the loss of 17 of their own, the vast majority of enemy aircraft falling to No 85 Squadron based at West Malling. This unit was particularly effective against the FW190 fighter-bombers that had started operating under the cover of darkness. Though more difficult to intercept than the Ju88s and Do217s more usually encountered, the night *Jabos* fared little better against the Mosquito. As an example, No 85 claimed an impressive 'bag' of four Focke-Wulfs destroyed and one probable over the South Coast on the night of 16/17 May.

Below:
Flight Lieutenant J. Pattison of No 485 Squadron, RNZAF, graphically recounts a combat to Squadron Leader 'Reg' Grant (left), and Flight Lieutenant R. Baker (right), Westhampnett, 21 January 1943. The New Zealanders formed part of the Tangmere Wing, flying Ramrods with their Spitfire Vs. These three pilots had completed 279 operational sorties between them; and Grant, who had risen from sergeant to squadron leader in six months, had six kills to his credit.
CH 8385

Many Beaufighter and Mosquito squadrons were now also participating in offensive operations, taking the war to the Luftwaffe and striking at enemy transport and other ground targets. In the spring the Mosquito VI fighter-bomber became available, able to carry a useful bomb-load or extra fuel in addition to its normal armament. The Mk VI would become the principal offensive variant of the 'Wooden Wonder'. Some squadrons also assisted Coastal Command on daylight 'Instep' patrols over the Bay of Biscay, seeking out the Ju88 fighters that preyed on RAF aircraft engaged on anti-submarine duties or transiting to Gibraltar. Others were involved in the increasingly important activity of bomber support. In June Nos 456 and 605 Squadrons commenced 'Flower' sorties, attacking enemy night-fighter airfields — or patrolling in their vicinity — during Bomber Command raids. No 25 Squadron pioneered 'Mahmoud' operations, in which Mosquitos fitted with AI Mk IV and 'Monica' tail warning radar flew with the RAF bomber streams and attempted to lure German night-fighters into combat. Beaufighters of No 141 Squadron flew sorties over airfields in the Netherlands, using a device called 'Serrate' which homed in on the transmissions from Luftwaffe AI radar. Effective though they were at disrupting enemy activity, these operations were not without cost — 52 Mosquitos and 13 Beaufighters were lost during the course of the year.

While the Mosquito had the endurance to penetrate deep into enemy airspace, the Spitfire's lack of range was severely hampering daylight escort operations. This was most apparent when supporting the Americans, whose B-17s and B-24s were now flying regularly against long-range targets in Germany and occupied Europe — well beyond the limited reach of the RAF fighters. It was particularly galling for the British pilots to have to abandon their charges over Belgium or the Netherlands, only to rendezvous with them on the return leg and witness shot-up bombers limping home, sometimes with dead and wounded aboard. Various experiments had already been carried out with jettisonable auxiliary fuel tanks, and 'slipper' tanks of various capacities were now in use. Even with these, however, the Spitfire IX's radius of action was limited to between 240 and 270 miles from base, and certainly no further than the German border.

The one single-seat aircraft in RAF service that did have an adequate radius of action was the North American Mustang I, an aircraft originally designed for British use but rejected as a fighter on account of its poor performance at altitude. From February 1942 Mustangs had been operating with Army Co-operation Command, undertaking low-level photo-reconnaissance sorties, anti-shipping patrols and Rhubarbs. The first sorties over Germany were flown in October of that year. When the Mustang's airframe was later mated to a Rolls-Royce Merlin engine, the result was an aircraft destined to become the outstanding escort fighter of the war, possessed of a phenomenal range and the performance to match any opposing aircraft. Yet even with its original un-supercharged Allison engine, the Mustang I was faster than the FW190 between 5,000 and 15,000ft, and had a diving performance similar to the German fighter. In view of the losses suffered by RAF bombers on low-

Above:
Wing Commander Richard 'Dickie' Milne, wing leader at Biggin Hill, in the cockpit of his Spitfire IX, February 1943. The 23-year-old pilot was officially credited with 13 confirmed kills at this time. He would claim one more before being shot down over the Channel by FW190s on 14 March. He baled out successfully, but was picked up by the Germans and had to sit out the rest of the war in a POW camp. **CH 8656**

level daylight operations, it is perhaps surprising that more was not made of this aircraft in the escort role, especially in view of the fact that its range was more than twice that of the Spitfire.

By the middle of 1943, most of the problems with the Typhoon had been ironed out and the aircraft was in service with 14 squadrons. Having done much to defeat the Luftwaffe's low-level 'tip and run' raids, most of the 'Tiffies' were now being committed to ground-attack operations, a role that had been effectively demonstrated by No 609 Squadron during the preceding months. With the benefit of 45gal auxiliary fuel tanks, which gave them a range of over 1,000 miles, Typhoons were able to penetrate much further into occupied Europe, strafing enemy airfields, locomotives and other targets. A number of squadrons operated aircraft converted to carry 500lb bombs, and these so-called 'Bomphoons' were particularly effective in strikes against airfields and coastal shipping. In October selected Typhoon squadrons began practising with the 60lb explosive rocket projectile, a formidable addition to Fighter Command's armoury, and one which during the invasion of France in the following year would become synonymous with the Typhoon and its new tactical-support role.

The Typhoon's predecessor, the venerable Hawker Hurricane, had largely disappeared from Fighter Command's front line. Only three full squadrons remained, all dedicated to ground attack. No 184 Squadron had formed in December 1942 with the Hurricane IID, fitted with two 40mm cannon. After experimenting with ground-attack tactics during the spring of 1943, the squadron converted to the Hurricane IV. This variant had the so-called 'universal' or 'low attack' wing, with capacity for bombs, rockets or cannon (two machine-guns being retained for sighting purposes). The squadron carried out its first operational sortie in June, using rockets against shipping off the Dutch coast. That summer Nos 137 and 164 Squadrons also began operations with cannon- and rocket-equipped Hurricane IVs, employing them on sweeps, Rhubarbs and anti-shipping strikes. Both squadrons took part in a memorable operation on 2 September, against lock gates at Handsweert in the Netherlands, during which three Hurricanes, and an escorting Typhoon, were shot down by flak. No 164 Squadron's CO, Squadron Leader D. P. McKeown, was one of three pilots killed. By the end of the year all three Hurricane squadrons had begun re-equipping with Typhoons.

The role of air support had now become one of the most important factors in the preparations for the opening of the Second Front. The Dieppe fiasco in 1942 had demonstrated to the planners the crucial value of air superiority, not only over the beach-head itself but far enough beyond to prevent the enemy concentrating his own air strength. During the North African campaign the fighters and light bombers of the Desert Air Force had performed admirably in support of Montgomery's Eighth Army, and showed the value of effective air-to-ground co-operation. At home a large-scale combined-services exercise in March 1943 — Operation 'Spartan' — provided a further opportunity to test the tactics of mobile air support. The clear message now being assimilated was that the efforts of all RAF commands — even the heavy bombers — should be made available in order to assist the ground forces in securing their objectives.

This broader concept of air power was manifested by major organisational changes that began in the middle of 1943, designed to provide the forthcoming invasion of Europe with adequate aerial cover and offensive firepower. On 1 June Bomber Command's No 2 Group, which contained all the RAF's light and medium day bombers, was transferred to Fighter Command. In the same month, Army Co-operation Command was disbanded and all of its squadrons, including the valuable Mustang fighter-reconnaissance force, also assigned to Fighter Command. Two new 'composite' groups — No 83 and No 84 — were now established on paper, each comprising fighters, fighter-bombers and tactical-reconnaissance aircraft. Together with the bombers of No 2 Group, they would form the basis of a new tactical air force that would directly support the British and Canadian armies on the Continent.

As part of these developments, major changes were made to the ground organisation of those units earmarked for the Second Front. Squadrons were to consist only of their aircraft and aircrew, the ground staff being separated and formed into independent servicing echelons, able to deal with different aircraft types in primitive conditions. Groups of two or three squadrons were assigned to various numbered units called 'airfields' (later reclassified as wings), with a core of headquarters and administrative personnel. They were designed to function in a mobile role on advanced landing strips near to the battlefront. As further preparation for the coming events, tents had replaced more permanent accommodation, and during the summer months, at least, many of the personnel involved had been getting used to a life under canvas!

Until the invasion could be launched, however, the RAF's fighter squadrons remained under the control of their existing groups, and there was no let-up in the pace or variety of operations. The Spitfire squadrons continued to support the Eighth Air Force's deep-penetration raids, and to escort No 2 Group on Ramrods against targets in France and the Low Countries. By now the RAF medium bombers had been joined by US B-26 Marauder units, which had begun operations in May. American fighter groups based in Britain were also growing in size and reach. The upsurge in Allied bombing attacks prompted a major reinforcement of the Luftwaffe in the West, but the enemy fighters proved increasingly reluctant to engage the Allied escorts, preferring to wait for opportunities to tackle the bombers unmolested. Meanwhile, the Typhoons continued to target coastal shipping, enemy airfields and communications, and the Mustangs kept up their valuable armed reconnaissance sorties and Rhubarbs. As ever, these low-level operations were particularly dangerous — 126 Typhoons and 56 Mustangs were lost in the last six months of the year.

On 15 November Fighter Command was officially disbanded. Nos 83 and 84 Groups, No 2 Group and various photo-reconnaissance squadrons became the 2nd Tactical Air Force (2nd TAF). The remaining defensive elements of Fighter Command were formed into a new organisation with a resurrected name — Air Defence of Great Britain (ADGB). Both 2nd TAF and ADGB joined the newly activated US Ninth Air Force under an umbrella organisation called the Allied Expeditionary Air Force (AEAF), to be commanded by Air Chief Marshal Sir Trafford Leigh-Mallory.

A new development at the end of the year was the initiation of attacks on 'Noball' targets in France. These were sites associated with the manufacture, storage and launching of Hitler's 'vengeance weapon', the V-1 flying bomb. The true nature of these objectives was at first kept secret from all but a few individuals; the new device, still months away from operational use, would not be launched against Britain until the following summer. Throughout the winter of 1943/4, Noball sites remained a priority target for the Typhoon dive-bomber squadrons, as well as the Allied medium and heavy bombers. This apart, however, there was now really only one preoccupation in the Allied camp. The invasion, which all knew must occur somewhere in France in the spring of 1944, was no longer a distant prospect. The vast build-up of men and *matériel* had been set in motion, and the role of the RAF's fighter force in the great endeavour had been mapped out.

Above: Squadron Leader Stanislaw Lapka, CO of No 302 'City of Poznan' Squadron, is helped into his parachute by his ground crew at Kirton-in-Lindsey, March 1943. His aircraft, Spitfire VB EN865/WX-L, wears the Polish national insignia and the squadron badge — featuring a stylised raven — below the cockpit. A small piece of tape has been stuck over the '302' at the base of the diamond, to hide the squadron's identity from the camera! **HU 86389**

Above: As ground staff work on another Spitfire, Squadron Leader Lapka roars low over the airfield for the benefit of the photographer. A third aircraft can be seen in the background, tucked into its brick and earth blast pen. No 302 Squadron spent an uneventful spring in Lincolnshire and Yorkshire, before heading south again to take part in sweeps and escorts. It eventually re-equipped with Mk IXs and joined the Polish Wing at Northolt. **HU 87562**

Above: Whirlwind pilots of No 137 Squadron at Manston, 5 March 1943. The group is led by Squadron Leader H. St J. Coghlan, and the unit's bull mastiff mascot, 'Lynn'. No 137 was the second of the two Whirlwind squadrons in Fighter Command, and along with No 263 was engaged on anti-shipping and ground-attack operations along the coast of France. **HU 86319**

Right:
One of No 137 Squadron's Whirlwinds (P7012) is re-armed with 250lb bombs. Locomotives were a favourite target for the 'Whirlibombers', and the squadron had claimed 37 in six months of day and night operations. In June the Whirlwinds were exchanged for Hurricane IVs. By the end of the year both Whirlwind squadrons had begun converting to Typhoons. This is another picture to have received attention from the censor. **HU 87720**

Above: A cheerful Squadron Leader Don Kingaby, commanding No 122 'Bombay' Squadron, seated in the cockpit of his Spitfire IX at Hornchurch, 11 March 1943. His aircraft bears the squadron's emblem, a leopard on a blue star, as well as an impressive tally of 22 kills, nearly all of which were enemy fighters. Kingaby took up a staff appointment at Fighter Command HQ later in the year, and was able to add to his score only once more, over Normandy in 1944. **HU 87561**

Above: The first variant of the Mosquito to carry centimetric radar was the Mk XII, of which 97 were built, all converted from Mk IIs. The parabolic focusing dish and transmitter/ receiver aerial for its AI Mk VIII radar were housed in a plastic 'thimble nose' radome. The nose machine-guns had to be removed, but the four 20mm cannon in its belly gave this Mosquito a powerful enough bite. Mk XIIs first equipped No 85 Squadron in March 1943, and were delivered to five other squadrons during the year. HK117, seen here, served with No 29 Squadron. **ATP 12184B**

Above: A Spitfire V of No 412 'Falcon' Squadron, RCAF, stages a mock strafing attack against 'enemy' troops during Exercise 'Spartan', 11 March 1943. This large-scale combined services exercise — the biggest of the war — featured two opposing forces, 'Eastland' and 'Southland'. Among many other things, it tested how well RAF fighter squadrons could operate in a mobile, tactical role — information of vital importance to those planning the Second Front. **H 27934**

Above: Also involved in Exercise 'Spartan' were these Typhoons of No 183 Squadron, photographed at Cranfield some time between 27 February and 9 March. The aircraft bear white temporary exercise markings on their forward fuselages. The Typhoons formed part of the defending 'Eastland' force, playing the role of enemy fighter-bombers. **CH 18119**

Above: Beaufighter VIF V8748/ZJ-R of No 96 Squadron being re-armed at Honily, 23 March 1943. The armourers are feeding belts of ball and high-explosive incendiary ammunition into the magazines of the aircraft's four 20mm Hispano cannon. No 96 Squadron was formed at the end of 1940 for night defence duties, but contacts with the Luftwaffe over Britain had all but dried up by the spring of 1943. The aircraft is painted in the dark green and medium sea grey camouflage specified for night-fighters in October 1942. **CE 22**

Above: Three senior members of No 610 'County of Chester' Squadron's ground staff with a Spitfire V undergoing a routine inspection at Westhampnett, 11 April 1943. Corporal Houseman (top), Corporal Phenna (with oil can) and Sergeant Moore (below) had all been with the auxiliary squadron since its formation in February 1936 (typically, first names were not recorded). The knowledge and experience of such men contributed massively to the efficiency of any unit. **CH 9248**

Right:
The modelling medic. Flight Lieutenant J. G. Eadie, medical officer at No 11 Group headquarters at Uxbridge, photographed with part of his miniature air force on 16 April 1943. The young doctor's collection of model aircraft apparently contained an example of every major type then in use with the Royal Air Force. **CH 9234**

Below:
Mustang I AP247 of No 4 Squadron, Army Co-operation Command, April 1943. The tactical-reconnaissance force was transferred to Fighter Command in June, ultimately to form part of 2nd TAF. Although dedicated to low-level photo-reconnaissance (using an oblique camera mounted in the cockpit behind the pilot), Mustang carried out harassing attacks on ground and shipping targets as well. Rangers became increasingly important during 1943, and five squadrons were still operational with the type in June 1944. **CH 9308**

Above: Ground staff wheel out Typhoon IB EK183/US-A of No 56 Squadron at Matlaske, 21 April 1943, the day the aircraft was officially revealed to the press. The Typhoon was then in service with 18 Fighter Command squadrons, though not all were operational. It had established itself as an effective counter to the Luftwaffe's low-level fighter-bomber raids, and was increasingly being used for ground-attack and intruder operations over enemy territory. **HU 86320**

Above: 'B' Flight, No 130 Squadron, dispersed at Ballyhalbert, Northern Ireland, April/ May 1943. The Spitfire V in the foreground was the usual mount of French pilot Lieutenant Jacques Andrieuz, who had claimed his first confirmed kill — an FW190 — in February. 'Jaco' Andrieuz went on to destroy five more enemy aircraft while serving with other squadrons. **HU 64362**

Above:
A Spitfire IX of the Free French No 341 'Alsace' Squadron, undergoing gun harmonisation in a blister hangar at Biggin Hill, 1 May 1943. An armourer can be seen using a periscope to align one of the aircraft's four Browning machine-guns with the relevant outer white spot on the harmonisation board, set exactly 50yd away.
The 20mm cannon were aligned with the larger black circles, and the gun camera with the centre white circle. This ensured that fire from the Spitfire's weapons would converge at a point 250yd in front of the aircraft, for maximum destructive effect. **CH 18603**

Above: Typhoon IB DN406/PR-F of No 609 Squadron at Manston, 14 May 1943. No 609 was one of the foremost Typhoon squadrons. As well as taking part in routine anti-*Jabo* patrols over the South Coast, the unit pioneered Typhoon day and night offensive operations under the direction of its innovative CO, Squadron Leader Roland Beamont. This aircraft alone had 18 locomotive 'kills' to its credit. **CH 9824**

Above: Squadron Leader Edward 'Jack' Charles, commanding No 611 Squadron, chalks up the Biggin Hill Sector's 1,000th enemy aircraft (shot down since Dunkirk), following a successful sweep over Normandy on 15 May 1943. That afternoon, Charles shot down two FW190s, while the CO of No 341 Squadron, Commandant René Mouchotte, destroyed another on the same operation. As it was not clear which of the two pilots had secured the 1,000th kill, the honours — and sweepstake of £300 — were shared between them. **CH 9990**

Above: VIP escort. Spitfire LF VBs of No 303 Squadron photographed from General Sir Bernard Montgomery's personal B-17 Flying Fortress on 17 May 1943. 'Monty' was on his way home for a short spell of leave following his victory over Axis forces in North Africa. The foreground aircraft, BM144/RF-H 'Halszka', was flown by Squadron Leader Zygmunt Bienkowski. **NAM 16**

Left:
The crew of a Mosquito II of No 605 Squadron climb aboard their aircraft at the start of another nocturnal sortie from Castle Camps, 20 May 1943. No 605 was re-formed in June 1942 as a specialist intruder unit, equipped at first with Bostons and Havocs. The squadron's first successful Mosquito operation was on the night of 4/5 May 1943 when two Do217s were shot down over the Netherlands. **HU 87564**

Left:
This close-up view of the Mosquito seen in the previous photograph shows just how cramped the cockpit of this aircraft was. The navigator sat on the right of — and slightly behind — the pilot. Their proximity to each other allowed good communication and was useful in an emergency. Unlike the bomber versions, Mosquito fighters had a flat bullet-proof windscreen. Mk IIs used in the intruder role had their AI Mk IV radar removed, but carried extra fuel for extended patrolling over enemy territory. **HU 87563**

Right:
The most numerous Mosquito variant was the Mk VI fighter-bomber, which combined the strengthened wing of the Mk IV bomber with the armament of the Mk II fighter. It could also carry two 500lb bombs or extra fuel tanks internally, with another pair of bombs or jettisonable fuel tanks under the wings. FB VIs first entered service with No 418 Squadron in May 1943, and were soon in widespread use with several night-fighter squadrons on intruder operations and Rangers over occupied Europe. HJ719 went to No 418 Squadron but crashed following an engine failure over Sussex on 25 June 1944. **ATP 12230G**

Above: Electrician was one of the many ground trades open to RAF airmen and airwomen alike (charging-board operator was a related but less skilled position available to WAAF recruits). These three are testing and charging aircraft batteries at Ford in May 1943. The fighter station's sole resident squadron at this date was No 256, operating Beaufighters and about to re-equip with Mosquitos. **CH 10089**

Above: Typhoon IB R8752 of No 1 Squadron, written off after crash-landing in a field near its base at Lympne on 2 June 1943. Flight Sergeant W. H. Ramsey hit a telegraph pole whilst on a Rhubarb over France, but managed to bring his badly damaged aircraft home. A week before, Ramsey had used this aircraft to shoot down an FW190 *Jabo* over the Channel. **CH 18509**

Above: The Hurricane IV was a dedicated ground-attack aircraft, heavily armed but appallingly vulnerable to flak and fighters. It saw action with only three squadrons in Fighter Command during 1943, but was more widely used in other theatres. These are aircraft of No 164 Squadron at Middle Wallop on 3 June 1943, shortly before becoming operational. The 40mm Vickers 'S' guns were soon replaced by rocket projectiles, but relatively few operations were flown before the squadron converted to Typhoons. **CH 10223**

Above: Mosquito IIs of No 456 Squadron at Middle Wallop, 5 June 1943. By now, the Australian night-fighter squadron had moved onto the offensive, strafing locomotives and intruding over enemy airfields. In July a number of Mk VIs were received, for use on daylight Rangers. Unlike intruder or bomber-support sorties, for which aircraft were assigned certain patrol areas, crews on Rangers were free to roam as far as their fuel would allow in the search for 'trade'. **CH 10317**

Right:
No 157 Squadron also partially switched to an offensive role during 1943. This Mosquito II is seen refuelling at Hunsdon on 16 June 1943. The censor has carefully obliterated the squadron code ('RS') from the aircraft's fuselage. As well as intruding and Ranger sorties, the squadron also flew a number of Instep patrols. In May 1944 it became a dedicated bomber-support squadron, joining No 100 Group, Bomber Command. **CH 10312**

Above: The end of this Ju88C of KG 40 was caught on the gun camera of Flight Lieutenant Joseph Singleton's Mosquito II, during an Instep patrol on 11 June 1943. Singleton was leading five Mosquitos of No 25 Squadron over the Bay of Biscay when they ran into a similar number of Ju88s. In the ensuing battle, one enemy aircraft was destroyed and two damaged. **C 3646A**

Above:
Typhoons of No 181 Squadron at Tangmere during a press visit in June 1943. Squadron Leader Denis Crowley-Milling's aircraft (EK270) is being bombed up for the cameras. Formed in September 1942, No 181 was the first of several specialist Typhoon fighter-bomber squadrons. Dubbed 'Bomphoons' by the newspapers, each aircraft carried a pair of 500-pounders, with which they dive-bombed airfields, factories and rail targets. Coastal shipping was also attacked, the raids often escorted by 'fighter' Typhoons. **HU 87560**

Right:
Back-seater. The navigator/radar operator of a No 125 Squadron Beaufighter VIF settles into his position, ready for another night patrol from Exeter, 14 September 1943. The plexiglass 'bubble' canopy was fixed, and like the pilot, he entered the aircraft through a hatch in the bottom of the fuselage. More likely than not, the sortie would be uneventful — Luftwaffe night incursions were few and far between during this period. **CH 11182**

Above: Flight Lieutenant M. Cybulski (left) and Flying Officer H. Ladbrook of No 410 Squadron, RCAF, with their severely charred Mosquito II at Coleby Grange, 27 September 1943. On an intruder sortie over the Netherlands the previous night the pair had attacked a Do217, closing to within 100ft before opening fire. The enemy aircraft exploded with such force that the Mosquito was enveloped by burning fuel and badly scorched. Debris also damaged the port engine, which had to be shut down (note the feathered propeller). Photographs of the 'toasted' Mosquito were subsequently exhibited in de Havilland's factories, as a graphic tribute to the strength of its design. **CE 106**

Above: Spitfire LF VBs of No 132 'Bombay' Squadron at Newchurch Advanced Landing Ground (ALG) in Kent, 1 October 1943. The serial number (AA850) of the nearest aircraft, named *Heather*, is just visible above the fin flash. No 132 Squadron was one of the first to join the newly formed 2nd Tactical Air Force, its principal task at this time escorting medium bombers on Ramrods. Newchurch opened in July 1943, one of a host of ALGs established in the South of England in preparation for increased fighter operations during the forthcoming invasion of Europe. **CH 11473**

Above: Exhibiting its aggressive lines to advantage, Typhoon IB JP853/SA-K of No 486 Squadron displays for the photographer during a visit to Tangmere on 27 October 1943. One of the Typhoon's problems, especially during its first months of service, was that it was frequently mistaken for the FW190 by 'friendly' anti-aircraft gunners and other Allied fighters. After various experiments the identification markings shown here, consisting of 12in black and 24in white bands, were adopted. **CH 11578**

Above: The nerve centres of Fighter Command were the group and sector operations rooms. This is No 10 Group headquarters at Rudloe Manor, at Box in Wiltshire, December 1943. WAAF plotters track the height and strength of enemy and friendly forces, while senior controllers watch god-like from above. No 10 Group's five sectors — Middle Wallop, Exeter, Colerne, Fairwood Common and Portreath — covered the West of England and South Wales, and at this time comprised 19 squadrons, plus a flight of Hurricanes based in the Isles of Scilly. **CH 11887**

1944

> *'To say the Allied air forces were omnipotent, omnipresent, overwhelming, is no more than the truth. That was precisely what they were. Leigh-Mallory swept the skies and carried all before him.'*
>
> **(Royal Air Force 1939-45, HMSO, 1954)**

By the beginning of 1944 Fighter Command had ceased to exist officially, its squadrons now organised into two separate entities — 2nd Tactical Air Force and Air Defence of Great Britain. The role of 2nd TAF was to provide offensive and defensive support for the British Second and Canadian First Armies on the Continent, once the invasion had got underway. ADGB, commanded by Air Marshal Roderic Hill, was charged with both the continuing defence of Britain and the aerial protection of the vast Allied invasion force now assembling in the southern counties. In January ADGB comprised 68 operational fighter squadrons, but many of these would be transferred during the spring to a massively expanded 2nd TAF. Commanding 2nd TAF itself was Air Marshal Arthur Coningham, who had led the Desert Air Force in North Africa with such success during 1942/3. He and his subordinates, especially Air Vice-Marshal Harry Broadhurst, in charge of No 83 Group, brought essential knowledge and experience of air-to-ground co-operation and tactical support, now such a vital part of the RAF's role, and on which so much would depend in the momentous year ahead.

Despite the organisational changes, individual fighter squadrons continued operations in much the same way as before, though there had been some changes. Circuses had long been abandoned — there was more than enough activity to attract an increasingly elusive Luftwaffe — and Roadsteads were now largely in the hands of Coastal Command. Ramrods and Rangers dominated, with sweeps, photo-reconnaissance sorties and the occasional scramble against enemy raiders mixed in. Attacks on Noball sites intensified, with the Typhoon squadrons heavily involved, while the Spitfire squadrons maintained their almost daily round of escort activities. The Spitfire was still the most numerous aircraft type in 2nd TAF and ADGB. During the spring many of those units operating the ageing Mk V were finally re-equipped with Mk IXs, although ADGB would still have 10 squadrons of LF Vs on the eve of D-Day. As the build-up to the invasion continued, units were rotated through various armament practice camps, where they honed their gunnery skills and learnt the art of dive-bombing. In addition, many of the Typhoon squadrons had rocket-firing techniques to master.

Development of the Spitfire was continuing, and the second Griffon-engined variant, the Mk XIV, entered service with No 610 Squadron in January. By June three squadrons were fully operational. Once again, the new aircraft was only intended as an interim type, pending the arrival of a more thorough redesign, but in the event was built in large numbers. The purposeful-looking Mk XIV was capable of 448mph at 26,000ft, and was at least 30mph faster than the Mk IX at all heights. Another new type which entered service early in 1944 was the Hawker Tempest V, the successor to the Typhoon, and, thanks to a thin elliptical wing, much more effective as a fighter. Able to exploit fully the power of the Typhoon's 2,180hp Napier Sabre II engine — now finally rid of its mechanical gremlins — the Tempest was manoeuvrable and fast. It could reach almost 440mph at 18,500ft, and was quicker than the Spitfire XIV below 10,000ft, a factor that would have important consequences later in the year when Hitler's V-1 offensive opened. The first two Tempest squadrons, Nos 3 and 486, became operational as part of 2nd TAF in the spring.

A third new aircraft type to make an appearance at this time was the Mustang III, the RAF's designation for the North American P-51B. Powered by a Packard-built Merlin, it had a maximum speed of 442mph at 24,500ft. Nos 19 and 65 Squadrons were the first to receive the new Mustangs, using them operationally for the first time on sweeps over the Netherlands and Belgium on 15 February. By the end of April six Mustang III squadrons were operational in 2nd TAF, flying a variety of escort missions. Such was the outstanding endurance of their machines, especially when carrying auxiliary fuel tanks, that the Mustang pilots were able to accompany the Eighth Air Force 'heavies' deep into Germany, usually acting as withdrawal support for B-17s and B-24s raiding such long-range targets as Magdeburg, Brunswick and Berlin. Operations were also flown in support of medium bombers over France and the Low Countries, and Coastal Command Beaufighters on anti-shipping strikes off the enemy coast.

The Mustang's range was exploited on offensive operations too. The first confirmed air victories were claimed by Nos 19 and 65 Squadrons on 22 April, when three Me109s were destroyed on a Ranger near Strasbourg and Nancy. On the following day four aircraft from No 122 Squadron had a field-day when they surprised a group of Heinkel He111s in the circuit over an airfield near Dijon, not far from the Swiss border. Six bombers were shot down and one damaged. In May several Rangers were flown over Denmark, one particularly successful operation on the 17th resulting in claims for 13 enemy aircraft destroyed, for the loss of two Mustangs. Like other RAF units, the Mustang squadrons spent time at the armament practice camps, developing their dive-bombing and ground-strafing techniques. It was intended that once the invasion started they would penetrate deep behind the enemy lines, and harass enemy reinforcements attempting to move up to the battle area.

The Mosquito squadrons spent the early months of 1944 combating Hitler's last-gasp night-bomber offensive against Britain, codenamed Operation *Steinbock*. This series of retaliatory raids, which came to be known by the British as the 'Baby Blitz', opened on the night of 21/22 January, when 92 bombers were despatched against London. Despite attempts to jam British radar, 25 of the raiders failed to return. The attacks on the capital and other cities lasted until late May, but the damage inflicted was minimal, and the Luftwaffe's carefully husbanded force — which might have achieved more had it been deployed against the gathering Allied invasion forces — was decimated by the defences. As well as repelling Operation *Steinbock*, some of the Mosquito units had a major role to play in the coming invasion. Six squadrons were transferred to No 85 (Base) Group, set up within 2nd TAF in March to take over the day and night defence of the Allied build-up area, and, in due course, that of the lodgement in France immediately after D-Day. Meanwhile, the Mosquito VI fighter-bombers of Nos 418 and 605 Squadrons — the intruder specialists — plied their trade deep inside enemy territory. Operations were by no means only carried out at night. Day Rangers, which normally involved pairs of aircraft, were sometimes flown as far as Poland or the Baltic — areas where the Luftwaffe least expected to meet RAF fighters!

In April, 2nd TAF began pre-invasion interdiction operations against the French railway system and other transportation targets, as part of a wider Allied plan to paralyse enemy communications in northern France. Fighter-bomber strikes were carried out against locomotives and rolling stock, roads, waterways and bridges. The fighters also played their part in a programme of attacks on enemy airfields, either by bombing and strafing them directly or escorting medium bombers to the same targets. In May a systematic series of strikes was launched against early-warning radar stations along the enemy coast, from Belgium to the Cherbourg peninsula, in order to render the Germans blind to the impending assault. The increased tempo of operations brought with it a corresponding surge in losses, mostly to light flak. For example, on 21 May no less than 30 fighters were brought down or badly damaged.

In the run-up to D-Day it was imperative that the air attacks did not inadvertently reveal to the Germans the intended location of the invasion. Thus the greatest weight of bombardment fell on targets north of the River Seine. It was all part of the complex deception plan intended to convince the German high command that the main Allied thrust would be against the Pas de Calais, with the landings in Normandy merely a feint. The fighter-bomber strikes against radar stations reached a peak in the first days of June, during which all the sites in the invasion area were knocked out. A few, near Calais, were deliberately left intact in

Below:
Squadron Leader The Reverend Hugh Storr conducts Sunday service before a congregation of fighter pilots in a dispersal hut at Tangmere, 10 January 1944. The 29-year-old padre was renowned for his boxing prowess, having previously represented Oxford University as a light-heavyweight. He joined the RAF in the summer of 1943, and soon set about organising — and participating in — a series of inter-station tournaments. **CH 12060**

Above:
Armourers clean out the cannon of a No 245 Squadron Typhoon (JR311/MR-G) at Westhampnett, 18 January 1944. Like most Typhoon squadrons, No 245 had converted to the fighter-bomber role and was now taking part in an intensive period of dive-bombing attacks against 'Noball' targets (V-1 flying-bomb storage and launch sites) in northern France. Rangers and medium-bomber escorts were also regular activities. **CH 12253**

order that a 'phantom' invasion fleet, created solely by formations of bombers releasing clouds of radar-reflective strips called 'Window', could be tracked by the Germans on the morning of the assault. The real fleet of naval vessels and landing craft assembling in southern ports was protected from the prying eyes of the Luftwaffe by the ceaseless patrols of No 85 Group.

The RAF fighter squadrons were about to play their part in the historic return of Allied forces to the Continent. The strength and composition of the force available would have been unimaginable to the pilots of the tiny Hurricane contingent that had operated in the chaos of the Battle of France, four long years before. The bulk of 2nd TAF's fighter and fighter-bomber force was controlled by Nos 83 and 84 Groups, which between them fielded 27 squadrons of Spitfire IXs, 18 squadrons of Typhoons and six squadrons of Mustang IIIs. No 85 Group had six Mosquito XIII squadrons, four with Spitfires of various marks and two squadrons of Tempest Vs. ADGB, the 'rump' of Fighter Command, now comprised a total of 39 squadrons, over half of which were based in No 11 Group. Three of its Spitfire squadrons had been temporarily attached to 2nd TAF, and many of the remainder would be called upon for escort duties and tactical support during D-Day itself and the first crucial days thereafter.

On the morning of 6 June 1944 Operation 'Overlord' began, with five Allied seaborne and three airborne divisions landing in Normandy. Both ADGB and 2nd TAF squadrons contributed to the huge air umbrella that covered the assault, with patrols over the invasion ports, in mid-Channel and above the beaches as the troops scrambled ashore. During the evening, other squadrons escorted the transport aircraft and glider trains which carried out the follow-up airborne drops on the flanks of the beach-head. Contrary to expectations, there was little Luftwaffe activity on D-Day itself, and only a handful of enemy fighters put in an appearance, but over the next few days the situation changed dramatically and increasing numbers were encountered. Enemy bombers made desperate and costly attempts to disrupt the landings, at first by day — 12 Ju88s were shot down attacking the beaches on 7 June — and then under the cover of darkness, when many fell prey to Mosquito patrols.

As the Allies secured and expanded their beach-head the Typhoons came into their own, hitting enemy tanks, gun positions and strongpoints with rocket-projectiles and bombs. RAF forward controllers attached to army units on the ground could use direct radio links to summon immediate air support from 'cab ranks' of orbiting Typhoons. Though vulnerable to enemy fighters when encumbered with bombs or rockets, the 'Tiffies' could look after themselves if the need arose; on 29 June No 193 Squadron was bounced by a gaggle of Me109s but succeeded in shooting down seven of their attackers for no loss. Meanwhile, Spitfires maintained defensive patrols over the bridgehead and carried out further escort operations, but the

Above:
Spitfire servicing at Hawkinge, 1 February 1944. This LF VB was serving with
No 322 Squadron, a recently formed unit manned largely by Dutch personnel.
The essential features of the LF V — the 'M' Series low-altitude Merlin engine
and 'clipped' wings — are shown to advantage. By removing the wing-tips and
substituting streamlined fairings total wing area was reduced by about 11sq ft,
which added about 5mph to the aircraft's top speed, as well as increasing
acceleration and rate of roll. **CH 12171**

weaker-than-expected Luftwaffe opposition meant that many units were released for ground-support operations, penetrating behind the German lines to strafe and dive-bomb enemy supply columns. The Mustang III squadrons were also deployed in a ground-attack role, striking at railways, river traffic and other communications targets far behind the front.

Though fighter opposition was by no means insignificant, light flak — sadly not all of it German — inflicted the majority of RAF losses, but at least pilots now had the option of putting down damaged aircraft in newly captured territory. Operating from across the Channel obviously ate into fuel reserves, and a priority was the construction of advanced landing grounds (ALGs) and emergency landing strips within the beach-head area. On 10 June the first RAF fighters landed at Ste Croix-sur-Mer, and within another 10 days eight Spitfire and three Typhoon squadrons were based in France. The landing-grounds in Normandy were primitive in the extreme, consisting of little more than some bulldozed fields, steel matting for the runways and a collection of tents. Many were uncomfortably close to the front line, and on occasion subject to enemy shelling and air attack. Waterlogging caused by unseasonably heavy rain affected some strips, forcing a number of squadrons to return temporarily to their Sussex and Hampshire bases. In drier weather, a totally unforeseen problem was created by the clouds of fine dust thrown up by aircraft operating from the makeshift airfields. It played havoc if ingested into engines, especially the Typhoons' Napier Sabres, and necessitated frequent engine overhauls and the fitting of sand filters.

Even as the Allies were consolidating their foothold in Europe, another threat appeared which caused a further reorganisation of the RAF's fighter squadrons. On 13 June the first V-1s (codenamed 'Divers' by the RAF and nicknamed 'Doodlebugs' by the British public) were launched against Britain. Each pilotless flying bomb contained 1,800lb of high-explosive, flew straight and level at up to 400mph at an altitude usually between 1,000 and 4,000ft, and fell to earth once the fuel for its pulse-jet engine had run out. The bombs, aimed at London, were soon coming over in large numbers (the daily average would be around 100), but had to face the combined defences of anti-aircraft guns, barrage balloons and fighters. Only the fastest aircraft could normally hope to catch a V-1, and consequently the Spitfire XIV, Tempest V and some of the Mustang III squadrons of 2nd TAF were quickly returned to ADGB control to deal with the new menace. They were organised into standing patrols and vectored onto their targets by ground control, picking them up visually for the final interception. Attacks were invariably carried out from dead astern, some pilots closing to within 100yd, although at very close range there was the possibility of their aircraft being damaged or even destroyed if the V-1's fuel tanks or warhead exploded.

The V-1 campaign reached a peak in early August, by which time 22 RAF squadrons were deployed in defence. Most effective were the Tempests of No 150 Wing, which destroyed 638 bombs out of a total of 1,771 claimed by fighters. The night-fighter Mosquito squadrons, some temporarily drawn from 2nd TAF or No 100 (Bomber Support) Group in Bomber Command, were responsible for the majority of night kills, knocking down a total of 471 V-1s. The top-scoring Mosquito pilot was Flight Lieutenant Francis Mellersh of No 96 Squadron, who finished up with an impressive personal score of 39. A specialised night-fighting Tempest squadron, No 501, became operational in mid-August, led by the RAF's leading Diver ace, Squadron Leader Joseph Berry, who single-handedly destroyed 59 bombs.

As the battle against the V-1 continued, the coastal belt of radar-directed anti-aircraft guns, firing shells fitted with proximity fuses, took an increasing toll of the flying bombs, eventually overtaking the RAF's own tally. The effectiveness of the combined defences meant that fewer and fewer bombs were penetrating inland. By September, with the launching sites overrun by the advancing Allies, the V-1 menace subsided. For the rest of the year the Luftwaffe kept up a desultory bombardment by air-launching the bombs at night from Heinkel He111s over the North Sea, but many of these lumbering bombers were shot down by Mosquitos and Tempests, and only a fraction of the V-1s launched in this way reached their targets.

While many of the home-based squadrons had their hands full dealing with Hitler's vengeance weapon, 2nd TAF continued to support the armies in France and maintain air superiority over the battlefront, which was now expanding massively. By the beginning of August, the Americans on the western side of the bridgehead had broken out from the difficult hedgerow country of the *bocage*, and were advancing into the interior of France. To the east, the British and Canadians were at last making headway of their own, having battled for so long against the strongest German formations. The enemy forces now found themselves trapped between US and British spearheads. As the Allies fought to close the pocket, Hitler ordered a futile armoured counter-attack against the Americans, which was smashed with the help of rocket-firing Typhoons. The German retreat eastwards became a rout, and the roads southeast of Falaise, choked with fleeing troops, armoured vehicles, lorries and horse-drawn transport, were strafed, rocketed and bombed relentlessly. On 21 August the Falaise pocket was closed, and the British and Canadians began pursuing the shattered German divisions as they headed north and eastwards towards the River Seine, harried all the while by the fighter-bombers of the RAF.

In early September the British Second Army reached Belgium, capturing both Brussels and Antwerp. The pace of the advance was such that the squadrons of No 83 Group, assigned to its support, had struggled to keep up. However, the ground forces were now halted by the complex series of waterways and rivers that blocked access to Field Marshal Montgomery's main goal, Germany's industrial heartland in the Ruhr. On the 17th, a major set-piece operation, codenamed 'Market Garden', began with Allied airborne troops descending on a number of key bridges in the Netherlands, the furthest being that over the Lower Rhine at Arnhem. RAF fighters escorted the transport aircraft and gliders, and provided ground support for the armoured thrust that now rolled forward along the airborne 'carpet'. Unfortunately, poor weather and poor communications restricted tactical-support operations by the all-important Typhoon squadrons, particularly at Arnhem where the bridgehead was gradually snuffed out by strong German opposition. Luftwaffe activity, which had fallen off following the breakout from Normandy, intensified during this period with attacks along the Allied corridor, and in particular against the vital road and rail bridges at Nijmegen. In the last week of September there were numerous engagements with enemy fighter-bombers, including the new Messerschmitt Me262 jets, and losses were heavy. Unfortunately the RAF fighters could do little to prevent the virtual destruction of the gallant British 1st Airborne Division at Arnhem.

After the failure of Operation 'Market Garden', attention switched to clearing enemy forces from the north and south banks of the Scheldt estuary, in order to open up the port of Antwerp for Allied use. This task was given to the Canadian First Army, which had been slowly advancing up the Channel coast, mopping up bypassed German garrisons in Le Havre, Boulogne, Calais and other ports. Supporting the Canadians were the Spitfire and Typhoon wings of No 84 Group, and in early October these began intensive dive-bombing attacks against enemy positions and gun emplacements along the Scheldt. The prime objective was the heavily defended island of Walcheren that dominated the mouth of the river. German resistance on Walcheren continued until 8 November, and the estuary would not be completely cleared until the end of the month.

Elsewhere 2nd TAF continued to fly defensive patrols and 'armed recces' (as offensive sweeps were now known), concentrating above all on interdiction sorties against enemy transportation. Operations along the entire front were hampered by the onset of unusually bad autumn weather, making conditions miserable at the forward airfields. The Luftwaffe was now encountered only sporadically, but during one action over Nijmegen on 5 October Spitfire IXs of No 401 Squadron shot down an Me262 — the first German jet to fall to the RAF. The recent appearance of this revolutionary aircraft prompted a return to the Continent of the RAF's own high-performance fighters previously involved in the V-1 campaign. Two Spitfire XIV and five Tempest squadrons were duly despatched to join No 83 Group. The Mosquitos of No 85 Group were also operating from bases in France and Belgium, but the inclement weather and decline in Luftwaffe activity meant a sharp reduction in the number of successful night interceptions.

On 15 October Fighter Command's title was officially resurrected, replacing the unpopular ADGB label. The change made no difference to the tasks of the home-based squadrons, which by now had virtually no aerial opposition — by day or night — to attend to. Fighter Command's principal function at this stage was to provide escort cover for Bomber Command, which had resumed daylight raids against German targets at the end of August. The medium bombers of both the USAAF and RAF, and Coastal Command's anti-shipping strikes in the North Sea, also required protection. The most suitable aircraft for the long-range role was of course the Mustang III; 2nd TAF's remaining Mustang squadrons had already returned to Britain to take up escort duties, and increasing numbers of Spitfire squadrons would convert to this superb aircraft in the months that followed.

A new Spitfire variant entered service in November. The Mk XVI was simply a Mk IX powered by a Packard-built version of the Merlin 66 engine. Many late-production aircraft also featured a cut-down rear fuselage and bubble canopy, a well-received modification that dramatically improved the view rearwards from the cockpit. It was the last major version of the Spitfire to see service during the war. Mk XVIs were used almost exclusively for ground-attack sorties, some of those with Fighter Command being employed against Hitler's last and most destructive 'vengeance weapon', the V-2 rocket. No fewer than 1,115 of these missiles, each carrying a ton of explosives, would strike British targets between 8 September 1944 and 27 March 1945. The V-2 could not be intercepted in the air, and the only counter was to attack its launching sites. Squadrons from No 12 Group were ordered to maintain standing patrols near

The Hague, from where the missiles were normally fired. The RAF fighters responded quickly to any signs of V-2 activity, dive-bombing and strafing the well concealed mobile launch sites, as well as conducting pre-planned strikes on suspected headquarters and storage areas. Almost 500 sorties were flown during November and December.

The last weeks of the year saw the Allied armies bogged down on the frontiers of Germany. German jets remained a problem, and three more Spitfire XIV squadrons were transferred to 2nd TAF to help counter their activities. However, the poor flying weather continued to restrict air operations, and an apparent lull in enemy activity seemed set to continue over Christmas. Then, on 16 December, Hitler launched his surprise counter-offensive against a weakly held sector of the American front in the Ardennes. Blanketed by cloud and mist, the Germans were unmolested from the air during the first few days, but were held up repeatedly by the poor roads and tenacious pockets of resistance. On Christmas Eve the weather dramatically improved, and the full weight of Allied air power was unleashed against the advancing columns. Typhoon and Spitfire squadrons played a major part but lost 21 aircraft, many tragically to American anti-aircraft fire. The Luftwaffe was also up in force during this period, but suffered heavy losses. A Canadian pilot with No 411 Squadron, Flight Lieutenant Richard Audet, became an 'ace in a day' on 29 December when he destroyed three FW190s and two Me109s. By now the German offensive had been broken, and the bulge in the Allied line contained. The Luftwaffe, though, had one last trick up its sleeve.

Above: The result of a minor mishap suffered by Typhoon JR328/JX-X of No 1 Squadron at Martlesham Heath on 6 March 1944. The aircraft's brakes failed on landing and its pilot was forced to swerve sharply to miss a parked vehicle. During a spell operating from this American fighter base in February and March, No 1 Squadron flew as close escort on US medium bomber raids, but its days with the Typhoon were coming to an end. In April the squadron moved to North Weald to re-equip with Spitfires. **MH 23662**

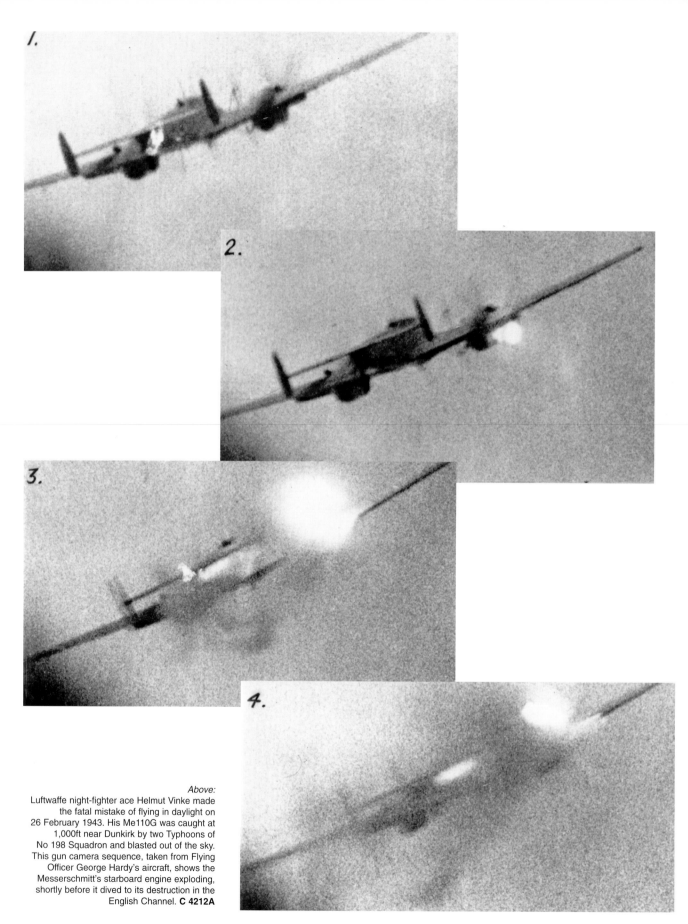

Above:
Luftwaffe night-fighter ace Helmut Vinke made the fatal mistake of flying in daylight on 26 February 1943. His Me110G was caught at 1,000ft near Dunkirk by two Typhoons of No 198 Squadron and blasted out of the sky. This gun camera sequence, taken from Flying Officer George Hardy's aircraft, shows the Messerschmitt's starboard engine exploding, shortly before it dived to its destruction in the English Channel. **C 4212A**

Above: Three in one night. On 19/20 March Flight Lieutenant 'Joe' Singleton and his navigator Flying Officer W. Haslam of No 25 Squadron shot down three Junkers Ju188s in the space of 20 minutes. Debris from one of their victims damaged the engines of their Mosquito, and the pair were forced to crash-land two miles from base. Singleton (left) and Haslam are seen with bandaged heads in the officers' mess at Coltishall in the early hours of the morning after their successful sortie. **CH 12519**

Above:
Back at Hornchurch after another operation escorting USAAF Marauders against V-1 sites, pilots of No 485 Squadron, RNZAF, cluster around a friendly WAAF dispensing tea, 30 March 1944. The squadron had recently attended an armament practice camp and its Spitfire IXs were in the process of having bomb-racks fitted, ready for dive-bombing and interdiction sorties in the run-up to D-Day. **HU 87717**

Above: The Hawker Tempest entered RAF service with No 150 Wing in the spring of 1944. This is JN766/ SA-N of No 486 Squadron at Castle Camps on 8 April. The Tempest V (the earlier marks did not go into production or appeared too late for war service) was faster than any other Allied or German piston-engined fighter below 20,000ft. It was also top secret — this and other official photographs taken at the time were not cleared for publication until October 1944. **CH 13956**

Above:
The Spitfire XII had been in service for over a year when this shot was taken on 12 April 1944 of two Friston-based aircraft from No 41 Squadron. Essentially a Mk V airframe mated to Rolls-Royce's powerful 1,735hp Griffon engine (which gave it a top speed of about 390mph at 18,000ft), the Mk XII was a low-level interceptor, equipping two home-defence squadrons. By 1944, however, enemy fighter-bomber incursions were rare and the Mk XIIs were being employed on offensive sweeps over northern France. **CH 12757**

Right:
Pilot Officer J. Allen (right) and Flight Sergeant W. Patterson, a No 96 Squadron Mosquito crew based at West Malling, survey the wreckage of the Ju88 which they shot down near Cranbrook in Kent on the night of 18/19 April 1944. The Junkers was one of eight enemy bombers destroyed by RAF night-fighters that night, during the last Operation *Steinbock* raid on London. **CH 12788**

Above: A Spitfire LF IX of No 313 Squadron undergoing an oil change at Appledram ALG, near Tangmere, 19 April 1944. Many fighter squadrons were operating from temporary strips in southern England, their pilots and attached servicing echelons getting used to 'roughing it' in the open as preparation for future deployment on the Continent. The three Czech-manned Spitfire squadrons flying escort operations from Appledram at this time (Nos 310, 312 and 313) formed part of No 84 Group, 2nd Tactical Air Force. **CH 12860**

Above: Production of the Allison-engined Mustang I and II was halted in mid-1943 to make way for the Merlin-powered Mk III. The new Mustang was designed for the air-superiority role, and finally gave both the USAAF and RAF a single-seat fighter that combined excellent high-altitude performance with an outstanding range (combat radius was 750 miles with drop-tanks). This No 19 Squadron aircraft, based at Ford, was photographed on 21 April 1944. It wears the standard Mustang recognition markings of white spinner, nose and wing bands. **CH 12877**

Above:
Pilots of No 132 Squadron with their CO, Squadron Leader Alan Page (holding map), and his Spitfire LF IX at Ford, 27 April 1944. Twenty-four hours earlier they had taken part in the first offensive Spitfire operation over Germany, strafing targets in the area between Aachen and Cologne. Page had been badly burned in the Battle of Britain, spending two years in hospital before resuming operational flying. He finished the war with 10 individual and several shared kills. **CH 12889**

Left:
One of Fighter Command's top night-fighting teams was that of Wing Commander J. R. 'Bob' Braham (right) and his navigator Flight Lieutenant W. J. 'Sticks' Gregory. Braham had shot down 19 enemy aircraft, mostly in Beaufighters, with another 10 claimed on daylight Mosquito sorties. Although the pair had staff appointments when this shot was taken at Benson on 19 May 1944, Braham still flew operationally whenever possible. It was on one such freelance excursion over Denmark on 25 June that he was shot down and captured. **CH 13177**

Above:
Development of the Mosquito in the night-fighting role resulted in a succession of variants. The Mk XIX was based on the Mk VI fighter-bomber and entered service in the spring of 1944. It carried either AI Mk VIII or the superior American-built AI Mk X radar in a 'universal' or 'bullnose' radome. MM652, photographed in May 1944, was delivered to No 157 Squadron, the first unit to operate this particular sub-type. **ATP 12807B**

Right:
The first Spitfires in France. Mk IXs of No 144 Wing at Ste Croix-sur-Mer (B-3) on the afternoon of 10 June 1944, the day the airstrip became operational. All Allied landing strips and captured airfields on the Continent were assigned a code number, a 'B' prefix denoting RAF control. B-3 was the first to be completed in Normandy and, despite shelling and the occasional sniper, was soon home to the wing's three Canadian squadrons (Nos 441, 442 and 443). **CL 88**

Above: One of No 144 Wing's control vehicles at Ste Croix-sur-Mer, after the advance guard of pilots had arrived on 10 June. The senior flying control officer, Squadron Leader J. G. Edison (with headphones), is standing in the back of the lorry. Seated to his left is Wing Commander 'Johnnie' Johnson, the wing leader. In the front, with some of the pilots, is the padre, Squadron Leader F. Lane, of Regina, Saskatchewan. **CL 89**

Above: Spitfires of No 132 Wing over the Channel on 12 June 1944. The nearest aircraft are from No 66 Squadron. All wear 'invasion stripes' and carry 50gal auxiliary fuel tanks. Air cover over the Normandy bridgehead was strictly controlled, with fighter units confined to specific patrol areas and times. This prevented collisions between the hordes of Allied aircraft in the air, and ensured that no gaps were left in the aerial umbrella for the Luftwaffe to exploit. **CL 108**

Above:
Typhoon pilots of No 198 Squadron at Thorney Island, 15 June 1944. 2nd TAF had 18 squadrons of Typhoons available for the invasion — 11 rocket-firing and seven bomb-carrying. By mid-June they were using ALGs in Normandy to re-arm and refuel, and by the end of the month many had made a permanent move to France. This aircraft, coded TP-T, is possibly JR197, which was shot down by flak near Cherbourg on 22 June, killing Squadron Leader Ian Davies. **HU 86371**

Right:
Armourers at Thorney Island assemble the Typhoon's most fearsome weapon, the 3in rocket projectile. The Typhoon normally carried eight RPs, fitted with 60lb high-explosive/ semi-armour-piercing heads. Rockets had four times the destructive power of the equivalent weight of bombs, but required a great deal of skill to aim accurately. The Typhoon's internal armament of four 20mm cannon was retained, adding further weight to the aircraft's devastating broadside. **HU 86313**

Left:
Typhoon pilots of No 181 Squadron leave the briefing tent at Coulombs (B-6) for another ground-attack sortie, 17 June 1944. Typically for pilots operating in Normandy, these dishevelled fliers are all wearing 'heavy duty dress' (RAF parlance for Army khaki battledress), with or without side arms and 'Mae Wests'. Maps are tucked into 1943-pattern 'escape boots', and some men wear sand goggles — essential for life on dusty airstrips. **CL 175**

Right:
Know your enemy. Flight Sergeant Morris Rose of No 3 Squadron points out the essential characteristics of the V-1 flying bomb to other Tempest pilots at Newchurch, 23 June 1944. The Scottish pilot downed his first 'doodlebug' on 16 June, and by the end of July had claimed a total of 11 destroyed. **CH 13428**

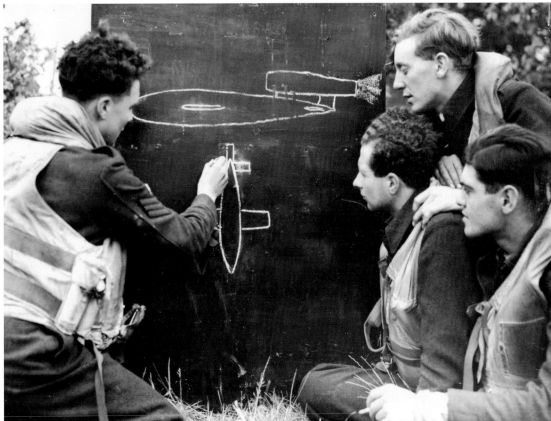

Right:
Ground staff re-arm a Mustang III of No 315 'City of Deblin' Squadron at Coolham, June 1944. The Polish squadron had converted to Mustangs in March, and formed part of No 133 Wing in 2nd TAF. Its staple fare of long-range sweeps, bomber escorts and dive-bombing sorties was interrupted in July when it was switched to anti-Diver patrols. The squadron would shoot down a total of 53 V-1s.
HU 86314

Below:
A German soldier stands by the temporary grave of Flying Officer J. W. Kelly, close to the wreckage of his aircraft. Kelly was one of two Spitfire pilots of No 602 Squadron shot down by FW190s over Normandy on 4 July 1944 (the other was Flight Sergeant L. H. Chaldice). The squadron lost four more aircraft that month, all to light flak while strafing ground targets. None of the pilots survived.
HU 3615

Above:
The Spitfire XIV was the second Griffon-powered version of the fighter to see service. Unlike the Mk XII, it was intended for combat at all altitudes, and was built in large numbers. The size of its five-bladed propeller is apparent in this view of a No 610 aircraft refuelling at Friston in July 1944. The squadron was busy helping to repel the V-1 offensive, and would claim a total of 50 flying bombs by the end of the summer. **CH 18184**

Left:
Australian pilots of No 453 Squadron help to flatten the airstrip at Longues-sur-Mer (B-11), 19 July 1944. Flying Officer D. Osborne and Pilot Officer A. Rice man the jeep while Pilot Officer J. Scott steadies the two 500lb bombs being used to add weight to a locally acquired agricultural roller. In the background, Spitfires of No 602 Squadron depart on an operation, watched by a runway controller working from a converted sentry box. **CL 509**

Above: Two flight mechanics refuel a Spitfire IX under the blazing midday sun at Longues-sur-Mer, 19 July 1944. Leading Aircraftman Ken Townsend passes another jerrican up to Aircraftman Robert Simmonds. The changeable weather of June had given way to hotter, drier conditions, and these two servicing commandos dress accordingly. **CL 510**

Left:
Flight Lieutenant Raymond 'Cheval' Lallemant's reputation as an admirer of all things equestrian was reflected in this shot set up in front of a Typhoon at Martragny (B-7) on 30 July 1944. The 24-year-old Belgian was a flight commander with No 198 Squadron at the time, and was soon to command No 609. Badly burned in a crash in August, 'Cheval' did not return to operations until March 1945. **CL 993**

Below:
With its rocket rails empty, a No 175 Squadron Typhoon taxies between the trees at Le Fresne-Camilly (B-5) after returning from another close-support sortie, 1 August 1944. By this date communications with the ground forces had been improved, and standing patrols of Typhoons ('cab ranks') could be called down when needed by forward controllers manning mobile 'visual control posts' in the front line. **FLM 1455**

Above: Final touches are made to the scoreboard on Squadron Leader Eugeniusz 'Dziubek' Horbaczewski's Mustang III (FB387) at Brenzett, 3 August 1944. The Polish ace was CO of No 315 Squadron, and a record of his 13½ aerial victories and four V-1s destroyed was painstakingly transferred to this newly delivered aircraft. On 18 August, in an engagement with FW190s over France, No 315 was credited with 16 kills, the highest number of enemy aircraft claimed by an RAF squadron in a single operation. Horbaczewski got three of them, but was shot down and killed in the same action. **HU 87719**

Above: Men of an RAF airfield construction wing sweating to finish off the 5,000ft runway at Lingèvres (B-19), 6 August 1944. Iron stakes are being driven in to secure the metal SMT (square-meshed track) surface, which was stored in rolls and had to be correctly tensioned to prevent it flexing in use. The airstrip took a mere six days to complete, and was the first to be constructed in Normandy by RAF manpower alone. **CL 709**

Above: Sunday service takes place in the open air at Lantheuil (B-9), August 1944. It was a measure of Allied air superiority that such a gathering could take place without fear of interruption. Three Canadian squadrons of bomb-carrying Typhoons were based here — aircraft of No 440 Squadron are visible. All were heavily engaged in attacks on the retreating German forces in the Falaise pocket during this period. **HU 87715**

Right:
Typhoons undergoing maintenance and repair at Melsbroek (B-58), near Brussels, 10 September 1944. An aircraft from No 247 Squadron (foreground) and a No 181 Squadron machine are parked in front of an elaborately camouflaged hangar at the former Luftwaffe bomber base. The Germans had gone to great lengths to disguise the airfield, fabricating fake houses, shops and even a chateau, all of which had failed to protect it from air attack. **CL 3979**

Above: Another Typhoon being serviced at Melsbroek on 10 September was MN627/SF-N of No 137 Squadron. This aircraft was destined for the 'chop' at the end of the month when it was hit by flak near Nijmegen. Warrant Officer M. Whitby successfully crash-landed his crippled aircraft behind Allied lines. **CL 3980**

Above: The Typhoon's devastating rocket armament was effective against tanks, gun emplacements, headquarters buildings and railways. Coastal shipping was another target, including this unfortunate tug caught in the Scheldt estuary in September 1944. In this case the shell splashes from the aircraft's four 20mm cannon assist the pilot in correcting his aim before unleashing a salvo of RPs. **C 4641**

Above: A pair of Spitfire XIVs about to set off on an early-morning anti-Diver patrol from Lympne, 29 September 1944. Although marked with No 130 Squadron codes, both aircraft had by this date been transferred to the Belgian-manned No 350 Squadron, which had recently moved in from nearby Hawkinge. RM619/AP-D was shot down by flak on an armed recce near Aachen on 16 January 1945. **CL 1353**

Above: 'Bombs for cigars — a good trade, wot?' Ground crew show off their stock of liberated 'smokes' as they decorate a 500-pounder at Eindhoven (B-78), October 1944. The Typhoon in the background, MN816, was on strength with No 438 Squadron, RCAF. It would be one of the many Allied aircraft destroyed on the ground during surprise Luftwaffe attacks on New Year's Day 1945. **HU 87718**

Right:
A corporal takes a break on the wing of Mustang I AL986/P 'Lazy Lady' at Eindhoven, October 1944. This No 430 Squadron aircraft was part of No 83 Group's tactical-reconnaissance component. As stocks of Allison-engined Mustangs dwindled, the 'Tac R' squadrons of 2nd TAF gradually converted to fighter-reconnaissance versions of the Spitfire and Typhoon. By the end of the war only No 268 Squadron was still operating the American fighter. **HU 87758**

Above: Dutch labourers use bricks to create a dispersal point at Volkel (B-80), 24 October 1944. In the background a No 274 Squadron Tempest (EJ714/JJ-W) taxies out for another defensive air patrol over the battlefront. Volkel was home to No 122 Wing until April 1945, when the Tempest squadrons relocated to bases on German soil. **CL 1452**

Above: What the Spitfire dive-bombers could do. Explosions straddle German flak positions close to the shoreline on Walcheren Island, 30 October 1944. This attack, carried out by Spitfire XVIs of the Polish No 131 Wing, was part of a sustained 'softening-up' campaign by No 84 Group and the bomber forces in advance of an amphibious assault on the fortified island. **CL 1482**

Above: Spitfire IXEs of No 412 Squadron, RCAF, await the start-up signal, Volkel, October 1944. Each aircraft sags under the weight of two wing-mounted 250lb bombs, and a 500-pounder slung below the fuselage. Though never designed for such a role, the Spitfire proved remarkably effective on interdiction sorties against enemy transport and communications. **CL 1450**

Above: The driver of a Church Army mobile canteen offers tea to a Spitfire IX pilot of No 165 Squadron at Detling, November 1944. The aircraft, coded SK-H, carries a 90gal auxiliary fuel tank beneath its fuselage. No 165 Squadron, part of ADGB, concentrated on escort operations until it stood down to convert to Mustangs at the beginning of 1945. **HU 87716**

Above:
Atrocious autumn weather turned airfields in Belgium and the Netherlands into quagmires. This No 127 Squadron Spitfire XVIE (RR255/9N-Y) has its daily inspection in a sea of mud at Grimbergen (B-60), 9 December 1944. Even the starter trolley in the foreground is receiving attention in this heavily posed scene. The 'E' wing fitted to Spitfire XVIs and later Mk IXs finally did away with the four rifle-calibre machine-guns, replacing them with a pair of .50in Brownings. On 29 December this aircraft was shot down by flak and its pilot mortally wounded. **CL 1699**

Right:
Not mud but 'spit and polish' for No 126 Squadron at Bradwell Bay on 11 December 1944, when six Spitfire IXs were ceremoniously presented to the RAF on behalf of the Persian Gulf Spitfire Fund. Squadron Leader J. A. 'Johnny' Plagis introduces members of his squadron to Lady Fowle, widow of Sir Trenchard Fowle, the former British Resident Minister in the Persian Gulf. **HU 86321**

Left:
2nd TAF rocket Typhoons could penetrate deep into Germany when fitted with long-range fuel tanks, in which case only two pairs of RPs were carried. Sergeant William Page (left) and Leading Aircraftman George Skelsey fit 45gal tanks to MN660/SF-K of No 137 Squadron at Eindhoven, 13 December 1944. The Typhoon was lost to flak on New Year's Eve, killing Pilot Officer J. Shemeld. **CL 1725**

Left:
Santa Claus (Leading Aircraftman Fred Fazan from London) hands out presents to Dutch children at Volkel, 13 December 1944. Members of No 122 Wing had saved their sweet ration for weeks, and contributed enough money to give the children their first proper Christmas party. It was noted by the photographer that this year Santa was afraid of Messerschmitts, so he decided to come by RAF Tempest! **CL 1729**

1945

> *'Anti-aircraft fire was now to be feared more than Focke-Wulfs or even Messerschmitt 262s.'*
>
> (*Royal Air Force 1939-45*, HMSO, 1954)

On 1 January the Luftwaffe launched a series of mass fighter attacks against 16 Allied airfields in the Netherlands and Belgium (and one in France). The operation, codenamed *Bodenplatte*, involved some 800 aircraft, a carefully husbanded force which had originally been intended for an assault on the American strategic bomber fleets over Germany. In the end, the Allied tactical air forces were targeted in an effort to relieve the pressure on the beleaguered German ground forces in the Ardennes salient. Approximately 120 Allied aircraft were destroyed during the surprise morning raids, but the Luftwaffe's own losses were fearful. Allied flak claimed many of the attackers, but others fell victim to poor timing; although some RAF squadrons were caught preparing for take-off, others were already in the air or returning from dawn patrols when the strikes went in. At St Denis-Westrem No 302 Squadron was landing when the attacks started, but following several minutes behind were the aircraft of Nos 308 and 317 Squadrons. These tore into the enemy fighters, claiming at least 14 of them over the airfield.

The two Typhoon wings based at Eindhoven were hardest hit during the assault, losing 26 aircraft destroyed or written off and 34 damaged. Eight aircraft of No 438 Squadron were shot up as they waited to take-off on their first operation of the day. The acting CO, Flight Lieutenant P. Wilson, was mortally wounded in his cockpit and another pilot killed as he attempted to get airborne. No 440 Squadron, also preparing to take-off when the Luftwaffe struck, lost its entire complement of Typhoons, although happily none of its pilots. Elsewhere, the German attacks were less successful. Only two aircraft were destroyed on the ground at Heesch, thanks to a spirited defence by the Spitfires of No 126 Wing, which shot down half of the attacking force. Some bases, notably Volkel, home of the Tempest Wing, were missed out altogether, and units from these were hastily diverted against the enemy formations. Despite the widespread destruction on the ground, British casualties were relatively light and only 40 personnel were killed, of whom 11 were pilots. By contrast, the Luftwaffe lost somewhere in the region of 300 aircraft and 200 pilots, including many of its remaining experienced fliers. Allied losses in *matériel* would be made good in a matter of weeks, whereas the German fighter force had suffered a major setback from which it would never recover.

By the end of January the Allies had regained most of the territory lost to the Germans during the Ardennes counter-offensive, but their own plans for the final assault on Germany had been delayed as a consequence. Though Germany was clearly doomed, the Allies' demand for unconditional surrender had been exploited by Nazi propaganda to bolster the resolve of the defenders, and the final battles would be hard-fought. In February Montgomery launched a major series of operations to penetrate behind the fortified Siegfried Line, clear the west bank of the Rhine, and close up to that last great barrier blocking access to the heart of the Reich. No 84 Group was assigned a close-support role over the front, and rendered particularly effective assistance to British and Canadian troops advancing against stiff opposition in the Reichswald. No 83 Group's task was to maintain the interdiction programme against transport targets behind the German lines.

Towards the end of the month 2nd TAF contributed to Operation 'Clarion', an especially concentrated 'maximum effort' by the Allied air forces against the German transport system. Railways, bridges, canals and road transport were strafed and bombed, but, as ever, the murderous flak took a heavy toll. Twenty-one RAF fighters were shot down or damaged beyond repair on 22 February, including no fewer than eight Mosquitos from Nos 418 and 605 Squadrons (both now operating under No 2 Group control). Almost 40 more aircraft were lost during further sorties over the next three days. Luftwaffe activity was extremely sporadic, but occasional low-level combats saw Tempests and Spitfires duel with Me262s, the new 'long-nosed' FW190Ds and late versions of the ubiquitous Me109.

The RAF fighters invariably came out on top in these encounters, in which inexperienced Luftwaffe pilots proved easy meat. Although a handful of German *Experten* remained, the Luftwaffe's fighter arm was but a shadow of its former self. Massively outnumbered by the Allied air forces, the *Jagdflieger* had endured many months of crippling losses, both in the air and on the ground. New aircraft were still being produced in large numbers, but the desperate situation meant that there was now little need for them. Pilot training had all but collapsed and the Allied strategic bombing effort had effectively dislocated supplies of aviation fuel. In the closing months of the war the Luftwaffe could do little more than offer token resistance.

If the Luftwaffe was now encountered only infrequently over the battlefront, it had almost vanished from the skies over Britain (manned aircraft not having been reported over the country since August 1944). The enemy's final incursions were made in February and March 1945, when night-fighters infiltrated returning RAF bomber streams and sought to attack the vulnerable Lancasters and Halifaxes on their landing approaches. To counter these last-ditch efforts, Mosquito night-fighters flew with the bombers, using various means to lure enemy aircraft onto them, before turning about and attacking. On the night of 3/4 March almost 200 enemy aircraft were involved in Operation *Gisela*, shooting down 25 RAF bombers but losing a similar number of their own aircraft. The three Ju88 intruders that crashed near RAF airfields that night were the last

enemy aircraft to fall on British soil. Attempts by the Germans to repeat the success of *Gisela* on the night of 17/18 March failed, and the Luftwaffe was never to appear over Britain again.

By the spring of 1945 Fighter Command's nine Mosquito night-fighter squadrons were engaged primarily in intruder and bomber-support operations — tasks they shared with Bomber Command's own Mosquito force in No 100 Group, and the six squadrons based in Europe with 2nd TAF. Many units were now equipped with the latest variant, the NF 30, which had a top speed of over 400mph at 30,000ft and was fitted with the powerful American-designed AI Mk X radar. Though on occasion still capable of inflicting casualties on the RAF's heavy bombers over Reich territory, the Luftwaffe's own night-fighter force had been steadily declining in effectiveness. The Allied advance in northwest Europe had gradually overrun its chain of early-warning radar sites, and American escort fighters, ranging at will over Germany, had taken a steady toll of its aircraft on the ground. RAF intruder and bomber-support operations continued to be extremely effective, so much so that during the final months of the war the threat of the Mosquito — whether real or imagined — was enough to cause severe disruption to enemy operations.

The home-based Mustang and Spitfire squadrons continued to escort Bomber Command on daylight operations to the Ruhr and beyond. The range of late-production Spitfires had been increased by fitting additional fuselage tanks, and units could now fly ahead to refuel at bases in Belgium and the Netherlands, rendezvousing with the bombers later. However, the long, cold flights, usually devoid of incident and with practically no aerial opposition, were unpopular with the pilots, many of whom would finish their tours without even seeing an enemy fighter. Ten squadrons of bomber-escort Mustangs were now based in East Anglia and, when not accompanying Bomber Command 'heavies', flew in support of Coastal Command Beaufighters and No 2 Group Mosquitos. The Mustangs of the Peterhead Wing in Scotland escorted Coastal Command strike aircraft on anti-shipping sorties off the Norwegian coast. In addition, No 12 Group maintained its offensive against the V-2 launch sites in the Netherlands, from where the missiles continued to be fired until the area was finally overrun in late March.

At the front the British began their last great operation, the crossing of the Rhine, on the night of 23/24 March. On the following day waves of Typhoons supported the main amphibious assault, and clouds of RAF and US fighters covered the huge parachute and glider drop on the far side of the river.

In contrast to events at Arnhem the previous September, 2nd TAF and British Second Army co-operated closely on the planning and execution of the operation, which on the whole progressed smoothly, although the flak-suppression effort was not as effective as hoped. The Luftwaffe rose to challenge the mass of activity, but could achieve little in the face of overwhelming Allied numbers. By 1 April US forces to the south had also crossed the river at various locations, and the Allies began advancing on a broad front. The last great obstacle had been breached, and the way into Germany was now clear.

Events now moved quickly. The aircraft of 2nd TAF started to operate from new bases east of the Rhine, with No 83 Group supporting Second Army as it began to encircle the Ruhr, and No 84 Group assisting the Canadians in their advance into the Netherlands and northern Germany. The Ruhr pocket surrendered on 13 April, and British forces pressed on towards Bremen and Hamburg. In these last weeks RAF losses were heavy — flak was still the main killer, but enemy fighters, mechanical failures and accidents all contributed to an average casualty rate of eight aircraft a day. There were plenty of targets, though, especially during the last days of the war as disorganised German units attempted to flee to Denmark and Norway. Naval craft, merchant ships and transport aircraft of all shapes and sizes were pounced on, as were the columns of vehicles packing the roads in headlong retreat. A detachment of

Meteor jet fighters from No 616 Squadron went into action over enemy territory for the first time, strafing ground targets but missing out on aerial combat.

The last day of action for Fighter Command and 2nd TAF was 4 May. Especially tragic were the losses suffered in these final hours. Mustangs escorted a Coastal Command strike off Denmark, but two aircraft from No 19 Squadron collided and crashed into the sea. Another Mustang, this time belonging to No 126 Squadron, was shot down attacking U-boats in a Norwegian fjord. A Spitfire IX of No 317 Squadron was hit by flak and exploded during attacks on shipping north of Wilhelmshaven. All four pilots — a Briton, a New Zealander, a Norwegian and a Pole — were killed. That evening a ceasefire was declared and the fighting in Europe stopped. On 7 May the Germans surrendered unconditionally. Suddenly it was all over, and the fighter airfields in Britain and in Europe at last fell quiet.

Below:
Gloster Meteor Is of No 616 Squadron at Manston, 4 January 1945. The Allies' first operational turbo-jet aircraft, the Meteor entered service with No 616 in July 1944, being employed against the V-1s. Despite its revolutionary power-plant (two 1,700lb-thrust Rolls-Royce Welland engines), the Meteor I's top speed of 410mph was below that of the Tempest or Spitfire XIV. **CL 2925**

Above: Squadron Leader Dennis Barry, one of No 616's flight commanders, in the cockpit of Meteor EE227/YQ-Y at Manston, January 1945. The other pilots are, left to right: Pilot Officer I. Wilson, Warrant Officer F. Packer, Warrant Officer T. Woodacre and Flying Officer H. Moon. **CL 3773**

Above: Snow and ice being cleared from a runway at Eindhoven in January 1945. In the background are brand-new Typhoons of No 182 Squadron — some of the replacement aircraft brought in to re-equip the squadron after the Luftwaffe attacks on 1 January. Despite losing nearly all its Typhoons during the raids, the squadron was operational again only three days later. **HU 87757**

Above:
After the snow came the thaw, and with it more problems for 2nd TAF. A pilot uses his dinghy to traverse the floods at Eindhoven, while a No 438 Squadron Typhoon (RB207) taxies past a roofless hangar, February 1945. Allied air attacks and demolition by the retreating Germans meant that few buildings were left intact at captured airfields. **HU 87753**

Above: A Mosquito XIII of No 604 Squadron taxiing at Lille-Vendeville (B-51), 1 February 1945. Six Mosquito night-fighter squadrons were based in France, charged with defending Allied ground forces and airfields from Luftwaffe attack during the hours of darkness. Between arriving on the Continent in August 1944 and being disbanded in April 1945, No 604 Squadron destroyed 32 enemy aircraft. **CL 1931**

Left:
In January 1945 a detachment of Meteor IIIs of No 616 Squadron joined 2nd TAF, for defensive sorties over Allied territory. This aircraft, still in its white winter camouflage, was photographed at Melsbroek on 6 February. In April the Meteors finally commenced offensive operations, strafing enemy ground forces and transport, but the war ended before they could be tested against the Luftwaffe. **CL 2936**

Below:
Typhoon prang. 'Babs VI', a Typhoon of No 174 Squadron, coded XP-K, was photographed at Volkel on 9 February 1945, the day after it was written off in a wheels-up landing. Like so many aircraft crashes, this one was down to engine failure rather than enemy action. The pilot was lucky to walk away. **MH 27462**

Above: Another No 174 Squadron Typhoon in a sorry state at Volkel, this time on 23 February 1945. This aircraft, bearing fuselage codes XP-P, is believed to have been hit by flak on 22 February, and was wrecked on its return to base. Note the wing armament access panels hanging open, and the No 274 Squadron Tempest parked in the background. **MH 27463**

Above: Armourers set the tail fuses on a clutch of 500-pounders in front of a weathered Spitfire XVI of No 603 Squadron at Ludham, March 1945. The bombs were destined for V-2 sites in the Netherlands. Rangers and interdiction sorties were also flown from this Norfolk location, but the advancing land forces would soon take the ground battle beyond the range of UK-based Spitfires. **CH 14808**

Above: In January 1945 RAF fighter markings were changed. Upper wing roundels were made more conspicuous, and sky spinners and tail bands were discontinued (to avoid confusion with Luftwaffe tactical markings). This photograph, taken at Heesch (B-88) in March, shows how the tail band of a No 401 Squadron Spitfire IX has been neatly painted out, using both upper-surface camouflage colours. For reasons unknown, a repeat of the aircraft's serial number is also being painstakingly reapplied. **HU 86323**

Above: Spitfire XIV RN119/AE-J of No 402 Squadron, RCAF, at Heesch, March 1945. The new style upper wing roundel, introduced in January, is clearly visible. The change to more visible national markings was intended to minimise errors of identification, usually on the part of American fighters! Note also the PSP (pierced steel planking) surface of the dispersal area. **HU 86322**

Right:
More Spitfires at Heesch, this time Mk IXs, which bear the 'Y2' fuselage codes of No 442 Squadron, RCAF. Unable to see ahead, pilots relied on an airman perched on the wing to keep them from running off the taxiways.
On 23 March No 442 Squadron left its Spitfires in the Netherlands, returning to the UK to join Fighter Command and convert to Mustang IVs. **HU 87759**

Above: The Spitfire's trademark elliptical wing was substantially changed in the Mk 21, a major redesign of the aircraft and the last variant to see operational service (with No 91 Squadron) before the end of the war. The Mk 22 and the final Mk 24 were essentially the same, except for a cut-down rear fuselage and 'bubble' canopy. All three were Griffon-powered, and had a four-cannon armament and a redesigned undercarriage. PK312, seen here fresh from the factory in March 1945, was the first production Mk 22. **ATP 13611C**

Above: German petrol wagons in a railway siding at Nordhorn under attack by rocket-firing Typhoons on 30 March 1945. Railway locomotives and rolling stock, river and canal traffic and MET (mechanised enemy transport) were the most important objectives of the tactical air forces during the last months of the war. **CL 2362**

Above: Mustang IIIs of No 309 Squadron line up ready to take-off on another long-range escort from Andrews Field in April 1945. Most aircraft are camouflaged but the two in the foreground exhibit the manufacturer's natural metal finish, now gradually being accepted by Fighter Command Mustang squadrons. **MH 6842**

Above: Another Polish Mustang squadron based at Andrews Field in the spring of 1945 was No 316, whose aircraft are shown at dispersal, together with a plentiful supply of drop-tanks. The squadron flew its last operation of the war on 25 April when it formed part of the escort for Bomber Command's raid on Hitler's mountain retreat at Berchtesgaden. **MH 6843**

Above:
Pilots of No 19 Squadron pose for a portrait with one of their new Mustang IVs at Peterhead, 20 April 1945. The CO, Squadron Leader Peter Hearne, is standing third from left in the back row. Famous as the RAF's first Spitfire squadron, No 19 had converted to Mustangs in 1944, and finished the war escorting Coastal Command Beaufighters and Mosquitos on shipping strikes off the coast of Norway. **HU 87754**

Left:
The war was virtually over when this shot was taken of a camouflaged hangar at Wunstorf (B-116), near Hanover, late April 1945. The airfield had only recently been captured following the Allied crossing of the Rhine, and was now home to No 126 Wing. A Spitfire IX of No 412 Squadron can be seen undergoing maintenance, surrounded by a miscellany of RAF vehicles. **HU 60608**

Above: The Mosquito NF 30 was the last and most potent night-fighter variant of this versatile aircraft to see action with the RAF. Two-stage Merlin 76/77s and a pressurised cockpit gave the aircraft an excellent high-altitude capability. It entered service with No 219 Squadron in the summer of 1944, and by May 1945, when this photograph of RK953 was taken, had equipped nine squadrons in Fighter Command and 2nd TAF. **ATP 13735B**

Above: Full circle. No 603 'City of Edinburgh' Squadron, Auxiliary Air Force, left Scotland in August 1940 to take part in the Battle of Britain and the cross-Channel offensive. Disbanded in 1942 to form a Beaufighter strike squadron in the Mediterranean, No 603 re-formed in the UK with Spitfires in January 1945, and finally returned to Turnhouse in April. Here some of the squadron's veteran ground staff watch as the City Arms are applied to a Spitfire XVI, 2 May 1945. **HU 87760**

Above: Spitfires into saucepans. With hostilities over, hundreds of surplus airframes were reduced to scrap. These Spitfire XVI fuselages being broken up at an unidentified salvage unit just after the war have serial numbers in the TD100 range, and bear the codes of the Dutch-manned No 322 Squadron. Note also the enlarged broad-chord rudders, which were a feature of late-production Mk IXs and XVIs. **HU 87762**

Above: Typhoon and Spitfire wings await disposal at the same location. Note the variations in size of the new upper-wing roundels, which have been painted over the earlier markings. The Typhoon, unlike the Spitfire, had no place in the postwar Fighter Command, and virtually every surviving aircraft was quickly scrapped. **HU 87761**

SELECT BIBLIOGRAPHY

Bowyer, Chaz, *Fighter Command 1936-68* (Dent, 1980)

Collier, B., *The Defence of the United Kingdom* (Official History, HMSO, 1957)

Cull, Brian; Lander, Bruce; Weiss, Heinrich, *Twelve Days in May* (Grub Street, 1995)

David, Dennis, *Dennis 'Hurricane' David: My Autobiography* (Grub Street, 2000)

Deighton, Len, *Fighter: The True Story of the Battle of Britain* (Michael Joseph, 1990)

Falconer, Jonathan, *RAF Fighter Airfields of World War 2* (Ian Allan, 1993)

Franks, Norman, *Royal Air Force Fighter Command Losses, Vols 1-3* (Midland Publishing, 1997-2000)

Golley, John, *The Day of the Typhoon* (PSL, 1986)

Gunston, Bill, *Night Fighters. A Development and Combat History* (PSL, 1976)

Hillary, Richard, *The Last Enemy* (Pan, 1956)

Jefford, Wing Commander C. G., *RAF Squadrons* (Airlife, 1988)

Johnson, Air Vice-Marshal J. E. 'Johnnie', *Wing Leader* (Chatto & Windus, 1956)

Mason, Francis K., *The Hawker Hurricane* (Macdonald, 1962)

Mason, Francis K., *The British Fighter since 1912* (Putnam, 1992)

Morgan, Eric, and Shacklady, Edward, *Spitfire: the History* (Key Publishing, 1987)

Ramsey, Winston G. (Ed), *The Battle of Britain Then and Now* (After The Battle, 1980)

Rawlings, John, *Fighter Squadrons of the RAF and their Aircraft* (Macdonald, 1962)

Richards, Denis, and Saunders, Hilary St G., *Royal Air Force 1939-45* (HMSO, 1954)

Richey, Paul, *Fighter Pilot* (Leo Cooper, 1990)

Shores, Christopher, *2nd Tactical Air Force* (Osprey, 1970)

Shores, Christopher, *Fighter Command War Diaries Vol 1 Sept 1939-Sept 1940* (Air Research Publications, 1996)

Shores, Christopher, *Fighter Command War Diaries Vol 2 Sept 1940-Dec 1941* (Air Research Publications, 1998)

Shores, Christopher, and Williams, Clive, *Aces High* (Grub Street, 1994)

Shores, Christopher, Foreman, John [*et al*], *Fledgling Eagles* (Grub Street, 1991)

Terraine, John, *The Right of the Line* (Hodder & Stoughton, 1985)

Thomas, Chris, and Shores, Christopher, *The Typhoon and Tempest Story* (Arms & Armour, 1988)